Bunny Guinness

garden workshop

Bunny Guinness

garden workshop

David & Charles

To John Courton, David Harrison and Martin Rodgers
for putting words into deeds.

A DAVID & CHARLES BOOK

First published in the UK in 2001

Copyright © Bunny Guinness 2001

Bunny Guinness has asserted her right to be identified
as author of this work in accordance with the Copyright,
Designs and Patents Act, 1988.

A catalogue record for this book is available from the British Library.

ISBN 0 7153 1090 9

Book design by Bet Ayer
Photography by Colin Leftley
Illustrations by Andrew Green
Technical editor Mike Trier
Copy editor Susanne Haines

Distributed to the trade in North America by
North Light Books
an imprint of F&W Publications, Inc.
1507 Dana Avenue
Cincinnati, OH 45207
(800) 289-0963

Printed in Italy
by LEGO SpA

for David & Charles
Brunel House   Newton Abbot   Devon

contents

introduction

Many gardeners are resourceful by nature and like doing things themselves. Using a jigsaw and screwdriver is no more challenging than mowing, hedge cutting or other gardening skills. This approach has the great advantage that it allows you to create exactly what you want for your garden, and hopefully gain satisfaction from making it as well.

The most effective and memorable elements in gardens are inevitably bespoke pieces. In *Garden Workshop* I have tried to demonstrate projects that can be altered to reflect your own style and adapted to fit your own requirements. When you buy something ready made, it is inevitably the same as someone else's – but when making your own furniture or objects, or having these made for you, it is always tempting to vary certain aspects. To this end various projects are shown with alternative finishes to encourage such flexibility.

The projects in *Garden Workshop* vary widely in their level of complexity, and the range of skills required to complete them. For those who are totally non-DIY orientated, there are a few simple, fun projects, but I hope that even if the thought of using a jigsaw or drill leaves you totally cold you can still pick up ideas for different elements in the garden and then cajole someone into doing it for you!

Finally, I have tended to use novel materials for many projects, in order to produce different special effects. If you have any difficulty in finding the materials you need, the suppliers list at the back of this book is very comprehensive and will point you in the right direction.

Bunny Guinness

general information

MEASUREMENTS

Measurements in this book are given in both metric and imperial units. Always work in one system or the other – not in a mixture of the two – as the figures given are not always exact equivalents.

Bear in mind that the majority of these projects involve the use of timber, and that timber sizes vary from one supplier to another. You should always check dimensions as you progress through the construction rather than relying entirely on the measurements given, which are for guidance and are accurate only for the timber sizes specified.

BASIC TOOLKIT

A list of the materials, tools and equipment required is given individually with each project. In addition, there are a number of items that we assume you will have, or have access to, if embarking on the type of work you will encounter in the book:

DIY Tools
Workbench
G-clamps
Steel measuring tape
Try square or combination square
Spirit-level
Handyman's knife
Handsaw
Hacksaw or junior hacksaw
Woodworking chisels
Electric drill
Set of twist drill bits 1.5-9mm (1/16 - 3/8 in)
Hammer

Screwdrivers, for slotted and crosspoint screws, range of sizes (*An electric screwdriver, or variable-speed, reversible electric drill with screwdriver bits, will save a lot of effort on all but the smallest projects*)
Pliers
Block plane or planer file

Gardening Tools
Fork
Spade
Trowel
Rake
Shears
Secateurs
Pruning knife
Pruning saw
Watering can and rose

SUPPLIERS

A list of the suppliers used for specific items in the projects is given on page 156, and a list of their addresses is on page 157.

SAFETY

Many of the processes that are described in the projects require safety precautions to be taken. Heavy specialist equipment, such as a chainsaw, drive-haul, or disc cutter, require training before use, or you might consider employing an expert for certain jobs. When drilling into masonry, wear safety goggles. With irritating or toxic airborne particles, always wear an appropriate mask (for instance, a dust mask when drilling stone or wood; a respirator mask when using spray paint or adhesive).

sculpture
in a hedge

This is one of the simplest projects in the book, requiring few skills and tools, but the end result is stunning. The supplier we used for the portrait 'sculpture' stocks quite a large range of torsos, busts and statues made from polyethylene; they are lightweight, durable and will take a wide range of paint finishes.

We have painted this sculpture with a proprietary verdigris finish but many other finishes would be equally suitable. Some suggestions are oatmeal-coloured masonry paint (as used on the finial on page 16), pewter-coloured paint, gold leaf or bronze paint.

This portrait head has been mounted on a length of copper pipe and positioned in a clipped hedge by pushing the pipe into the base of hedge. It could also sit in an alcove or on a timber or stone column; in these situations it would be better to weight it by filling it with a lean mix of sand and cement to make it more secure. Although it is a classical ornament it can work in a modern town garden or a very natural outdoor space. It also makes a great feature for a garden room.

MATERIALS

Moulded plastic portrait head
Copper pipe, 1.4m x 22mm dia. (55in x ¾ in dia.)
    or as needed
Expanding foam filler
Verdigris paints
Matt varnish
Matt black spray paint

tools and equipment

25mm (1in) paintbrush
White spirit
Respirator mask

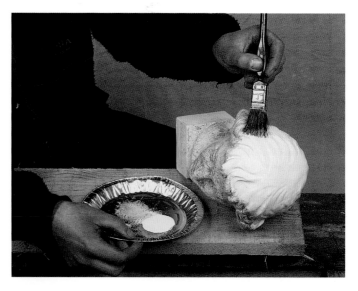

1 Take the hollow head and, using the verdigris paints (which are applied in three separate coats), mix the first coat and stipple it over the head.

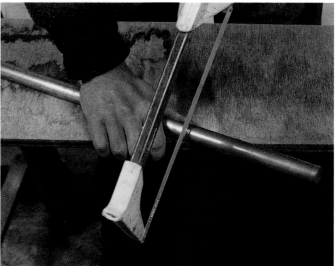

4 Cut a piece of 22mm (¾ in) diameter copper pipe to the desired length (in our case this was 1.4m/55in), using a hacksaw. Ideally, clamp the pipe in a vice to cut it, or clamp a block of wood to the worktop to prevent it from rolling.

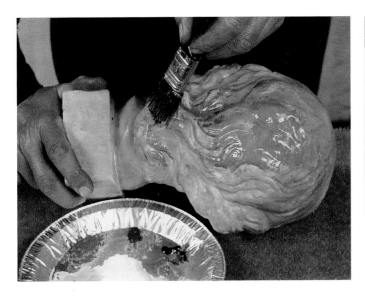

2 Allow the first coat to dry for 1 to 1½ hours. Then apply the second coat, mixed according to the instructions, and stipple it over the first coat.

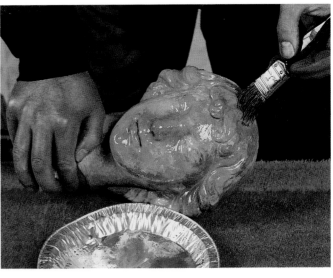

3 When the second coat has dried, apply the final, bronzy colour to the head, picking out the high points. When the paint has dried, apply a matt varnish.

5 Spray the copper pipe with a matt black spray paint so that it will be camouflaged when the head is installed. Degrease the pipe before spraying by wiping it with white spirit.

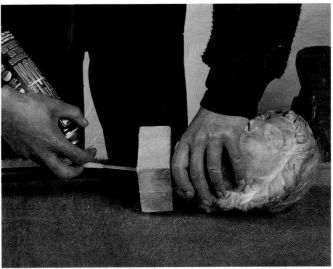

6 Moisten the inside of the head by filling it with water which is then tipped out. Push the pipe up the hole in the base of the head to the top and then, with the pipe positioned centrally, fill the void with expanding foam filler. Allow the foam to set for two hours.

finials

The use of finials in the garden provides a tremendous opportunity for adding originality and for stamping your garden with a special identity. They are usually positioned in eye-catching places – on top of fence posts or gateposts, on a building, or on piers flanking the sides of some steps. You could position one on a column in a flower border, on an attractive rabbit hutch or several around a pool to add a dramatic touch.

If you decide to use the more readily available shapes, such as balls, pyramids or ovals, you can ring the changes by playing around with scale and colour. For instance, ball finials can make a strong statement when used in an overlarge size to give a contemporary, bold feel to the space. In my garden I have used 600mm (2ft) diameter stone balls on 600mm (24in) stone piers instead of making the ball smaller than the size of the pillar, as is more traditional. Try experimenting with colours: finials are usually relatively small, so you can often get away with strong, unusual colours: turquoises, reds, yellows and metallic colours give finials an exotic feel.

Because of their often exposed position, finials must be durable and weather-resistant. Ideally, you should use hardwoods rather than softwoods, and select the more frost-resistant terracottas. Many gold paints will lose their metallic sparkle when subjected to wind, rain and sun and so, to maintain the unique look of gold, you need to use a high-carat, real gold leaf as shown on the fleur-de-lis.

artichoke

We made this artichoke from mortar in a pvc mould. It makes an ideal finial for wooden or metal posts on pergolas, fence posts or gateposts, and could easily be formed with a metal pipe in the base for fixing. We chose a fake stone finish but, with appropriate priming it could equally take gold leaf or any other colour. Alternatively, use one side only and set the artichoke in a rendered wall.

MATERIALS pvc mould; mortar, 1:3 Portand cement:sharp sand; PVA adhesive; silicone furniture polish; masonry paint; acrylic paints: yellow ochre, sap green, burnt umber, burnt sienna, Payne's grey; brush.

1 (right) The finial was cast in two halves, from a stiff mix of 1 part Portland cement to 3 parts sharp sand, with PVA adhesive added to the mixing water. Spray the inside of the mould with silicone furniture polish before casting. Join the two halves with undiluted PVA adhesive. Paint the casting with undiluted masonry paint of a colour to match the stone you wish to mimic. Allow the paint to dry thoroughly.

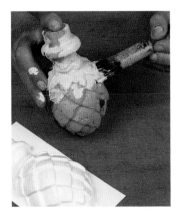

2 Using acrylic paints – yellow ochre, sap green, burnt umber, burnt sienna and Payne's grey – wash on the different colours, non-uniformly with a wet brush, to give the effect of aged stone with lichens and algae on it.

pine cone

This larger terracotta finial was specified for a big arbour in an ornamental, walled vegetable garden. To make it blend in with its environment we have weathered it down using acrylic and masonry paints; Winsor & Newton 'Finity' acrylic was found to give the best results. It would also make a good door stop for a garden door (though I would partially fill it with mortar for added weight) or could be used on a brick or stone pier.

MATERIALS terracotta finial; oatmeal-coloured masonry paint; green acrylic paint; brush.

1 Saturate the finial by soaking it in a container of water for a few minutes. Then when you are ready to apply the paint, brush on some more water so that the surface is wet.

2 Apply a coat of oatmeal-coloured masonry paint as a wash, by dipping the brush into the paint, then 'flowing' it over the surface with water. Allow it to dry thoroughly. This provides an effect of different tones.

3 To give the appearance of algae, wet the surface with water again, dab the brush into sap green acrylic paint, and spread it non-uniformly over the surface.

metal 'spade'

Ironwork is exceptionally flexible and can be moulded or wrought to form all sorts of interesting shapes. We have chosen an aluminium leaf finish which will retain the highly shiny metallic look, giving it a contemporary feel. The aluminium leaf comes in transfer sheet form, and is far less expensive than gold leaf. A more traditional look would be gained with black paint or gold leaf.

1 First prime the cast iron finial with red lead oxide paint. When it is dry, brush on a coat of acrylic size to seal the surface and provide a bond for the aluminium leaf.

2 Holding the leaf by the backing sheet, press it on to the finial with the fingers. Burnish it by rubbing through the backing sheet with a piece of slightly flexible plastic, such as a plant label.

MATERIALS metal 'spade' finial; red lead oxide primer; acrylic size; transfer aluminium leaf; burnisher.

wooden finial

This hardwood finial was designed and made by my local woodturner. We have painted it up using metallic paints, and applied aluminium leaf to the top sphere (see metal 'spade', above). The blue is a high performance opaque woodstain and the metallic paints are antique gold and pewter. Wooden finials fit into many situations. If you want to source some, it is well worth finding a local woodturner as they often relish the opportunity of making one-off items and will produce interesting pieces at very reasonable prices. In an appropriate situation, this finial could well have been used in its plain wood form.

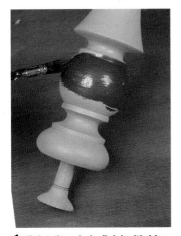

1 Paint the whole finial with blue opaque woodstain, then paint the middle sphere with antique gold acrylic metallic paint, brushing round the axis. Brush lightly so that the paint flows into a continuous, smooth surface.

2 Paint the bottom section with pewter acrylic metallic paint in the same way.

3 When both painted spheres are thoroughly dry, coat the metallic surfaces with clear acrylic varnish. Finally, apply acrylic size and transfer aluminium leaf to the shape at the top.

MATERIALS hardwood finial; blue opaque woodstain; gold and pewter acrylic metallic paint; acrylic varnish; acrylic size; aluminium leaf; brush.

lead pyramid

This pyramid was made to go on our trellis hedge house (see page 138), but here we have given it the lead treatment. We have used timber, but plywood would be a good alternative. Plywood can also be used to form two- or three-dimensional shapes such as stars, figurative shapes and crowns, and painted up accordingly. All you need is a bit of imagination and a jigsaw. Wear protective gloves when handling the lead and wash your hands afterwards.

1 First clad two opposite faces of the pyramid with lead sheet, cut flush with the angled sides and overlapping by 13mm (½ in) at the top and 20mm (¾ in) at the bottom. Clad the other faces to overlap them at the edges, by laying the pyramid on the lead sheet and marking the perimeter. Using a scalpel and straightedge, score a triangle 20mm (¾ in) outside the marked line.

2 Cut out the piece of lead along the score lines using a pair of tin snips, taking care not to cut inside the lines.

3 Apply lead sealant to the face of the pyramid from a cartridge. The purpose of the sealant is to provide a flexible bond between the lead sheet and the plywood.

4 Spread the sealant evenly over the surface with a spatula, so that there are no bumps in it.

5 Lay the lead sheet on the plywood, overlapping at the edges, and flatten it with a lead-dressing hammer. You can improvise with a length of thick dowel or an old rolling pin (not for re-use with food!). Bend over the edges of the lead and tap it into place gently, working from the centre of the face outwards, and along the edges.

6 At the top of the pyramid, neatly trim and dress the lead to form a flat apex for a ball finial. Connect the ball using a length of 6mm (¼ in) diameter dowel drilled into it and into the top of the pyramid. Glue the dowel into the ball with waterproof woodworking adhesive and secure it to the pyramid with lead sealant or mastic.

MATERIALS plywood or timber; jigsaw; guage 4 lead sheet; tin snips; craft knife or scalpel; straightedge; lead sealant; lead-dressing hammer; cartridge frame gun; spatula; small wooden ball finial; 6mm (¼in) dia. dowel; waterproof woodworking adhesive.

fleur de lis

Gold leaf is a stunning material, often keeping its brilliance for hundreds of years. It is real gold, beaten out into wafer-thin sheets, yet is suitable for outside applications. We have highlighted its versatility by applying it to a fibreglass shape, made in a pvc mould. This startling, gold fleur-de-lis would sit happily on a trellis gazebo, a metal fence post or an ornate garden seat.

1 This finial is made from glass fibre and resin, and is cast in two parts which are then joined together. Work in a well-ventilated area – preferably outdoors. Thoroughly mix the resin and hardener in the recommended proportions – and in manageable amounts – in a disposable dish.

2 Coat the mould thinly with petroleum jelly, to help in releasing the casting. Cut the glass fibre matting into strips. Pour the resin/hardener mix into the mould and press in the strips of matting with a brush, brushing up the sides of the mould. Mix more resin and hardener as required: the final thickness of the casting should be about 3mm (⅛ in).

3 When the resin has cured, release the casting from the mould. Trim the edges with scissors and smooth with glasspaper (a belt sander is ideal). Make the second half in the same way and join the two together with car body filler. Use this also to fill any gaps in the joint.

4 When the filler has set hard, smooth the joint and prime the casting in the required colour, using a paint suitable for glass fibre (for example, cellulose car body paint). Allow to dry.

5 Brush undiluted acrylic gold size over the surface of the casting and leave for the recommended time, until it becomes tacky. This ensures a light bond for the gold leaf and prevents slippage when applying it.

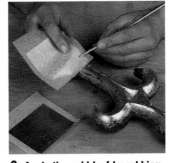

6 Apply the gold leaf by rubbing very gently through the backing paper on to the moulding, using a slightly flexible burnisher. A plastic plant label makes a suitable tool, or you can buy purpose-made ones for use with rub-down lettering.

MATERIALS pvc mould, glass fibre and resin; petroleum jelly; craft knife; brush; scissors; glasspaper; car body filler; cellulose car body paint; acrylic gold size; transfer gold leaf; burnisher (eg, plastic plant label).

galvanized steel planter

Metal plant containers add a contemporary look to the garden. If you make them yourself you will be able to create a range of different sizes, and they are far less expensive than ready-made ones. The container we made is about 400mm (16in) in height and diameter, but the method could be adapted to produce a much larger or smaller cylinder and the proportions can be varied. Larger pots are much easier to maintain, needing far less frequent watering, so I always tend to be over-generous when deciding on a size.

The galvanized bands could be increased in number from two to three if preferred, or else they could be painted with a metal paint after the galvanizing has cured, in contrasting bands of dark blue or dark green, or else picked out in gold leaf, aluminium leaf or copper metallic paint to make them still more individual.

Although these pots look decidedly modern, they can work well in a traditional garden, either mixed in with a variety of different pots or standing on their own. The choice of plant completes the picture: two pots either side of a Georgian front door may look more at home if they are filled with lollipop bays rather than with a thick clump of grasses, for instance.

MATERIALS

Galvanized steel sheet, 0.5 x 400 x 1280mm ($\frac{1}{50}$ x 16 x $51\frac{1}{4}$in) approx (ideally from offcuts)

Marine plywood, 18 x 500 x 900mm ($\frac{3}{4}$ x 20 x 36in) approx

Galvanized steel strips, 2 of 20mm x 1300mm ($\frac{3}{4}$ x 52in)

Mild steel edging section, size UF3, 1300m (52in) long (double this length if fitting to the bottom edge also)

Rope, approx 3m (10ft) long

Pop rivets, 3mm ($\frac{1}{8}$in) dia.

tools and equipment

Pop rivet gun

2 Mole grips

Jigsaw

Tin snips

High speed steel (HSS) twist drill bit, 3mm ($\frac{1}{8}$in) dia.

1 Cut two discs of 18mm ($\frac{3}{4}$in) plywood, 400mm (16in) in diameter, using a jigsaw. In one disc, drill two 12mm ($\frac{1}{2}$in) holes on the diameter about 75mm (3in) inside the circumference and knot both ends of a short length of rope through the holes to form handles. Lay the cut sheet of 0.5mm ($\frac{1}{50}$in) galvanized steel on a length of rope (to be used as a tourniquet) and bend it round the discs to form a cylinder. The ends of the sheet should overlap by not less than 20mm ($\frac{3}{4}$in). Tighten the tourniquet by tying the ends together and twisting a length of batten through the loop until the joint between the ends is fully closed. Check that the edges are flush, and clamp the overlapping ends together with two Mole grips.

2 Position one disc so that the outer face is 50mm (2in) from the edge of the cylinder, and the other about 20mm ($\frac{3}{4}$in) in. Drill through both thicknesses of metal, 15mm ($\frac{5}{8}$in) in from each edge, for a pop rivet.

3 Insert the stem of the rivet into the jaws of the rivetting gun.

4 Insert the other end into the drilled hole and squeeze the handles together. Release them to move the grip further along the stem and repeat until the stem snaps off. Rivet the other end in the same way, and insert a further rivet in the centre of the join if necessary.

5 Two bands of 20mm (¾ in) wide galvanized steel are fixed round the cylinder to give it rigidity. The rivets in one of these also anchor the base of the container. Drill holes for the rivets through the band, the first one centred 25mm (1in) from one end, the last one centred 10mm (⅜ in) from the other end, and the remainder at approximately 230mm (9in) centres between these. Position the first band 50mm (2in) in from the edge of the cylinder, with the 25mm (1in) end overlapping the outer layer of the join in the cylinder. Drill through the hole into the cylinder and rivet the end in place. Work along the band, drilling and rivetting through each hole in turn. The ends of the band should butt together. Fix the other band in the same way, then remove the disc which has not been anchored.

6 The cut edges of the cylinder are quite sharp. Cut a length of metal edging section to the exact circumference of the cylinder and push it on to the top edge so that it overlaps the joined ends of the cylinder. The bottom edge can be protected in the same way, if you wish, to avoid the danger of cuts when lifting the container.

7 Remove the knotted rope handle from the anchored disc – now the base of the container – and drill a ring of drainage holes, centred at the same radius as the two existing holes. A total of seven should be sufficient.

compost bins

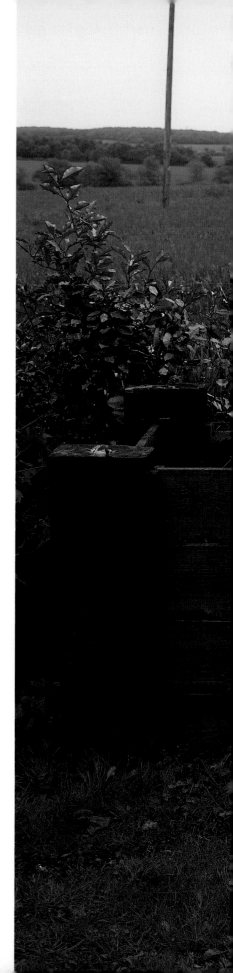

Compost is a must for most gardeners, but the siting of bins can cause problems. These sturdy bins need not be hidden out of the way, but can be tucked into an accessible corner, allowing you to utilize all your organic waste.

A set of three bins is useful, so that while one is being filled, the other two are at different stages of rotting. If you do not have much space you could easily get by with two, and one would be better than nothing. The bins are designed so that the sides will lift out, making it easier to turn the compost and empty it out. The gap between the posts (which are made from railway sleepers) is 600mm (24in) on the front and 900mm (36in) on the sides. The size of both gaps could easily be increased to 1.2m (4ft), making the bins bigger and giving lots more space.

We have shown three different styles of wooden sides – wavy boards, rustic logs and bark-clad timber – so you can choose one to suit your garden and your taste. The wooden sides consisting of wavy boards (opposite) would not look out of place in a modern garden, especially if a bright woodstain finish is used.

Sleepers are extremely heavy, and the cutting and positioning of them is awkward and hard work. However, once they are in place they will last a long time – a lot longer than the side panels, which will need periodic replacement. We have used imported hardwood sleepers which, surprisingly, are less expensive than the marginally smaller but lighter British softwood ones. Either will suffice.

MATERIALS

Railway sleepers, imported hard-
    wood, 4 of 2.6m x 250 x 150mm
    (8ft 6in x 10 x 6in) or similar
Batten, 25 x 38mm (1 x 1½ in):
    36m (118ft) approx
Cladding for side panels;
    three options:
–   Tanalized sawn softwood
    boards, 22 x 200mm (⅞ x 8in):
    33m (108ft)
–   Rustic logs, 70mm (2¾in) dia.
    approx:
    70m (230ft) approx
–   Bark-clad log strips, varying
    widths; assume average width
    of 100mm (4in):
    67m (220ft) approx
Woodstain, for softwood option only
Galvanized nails, 50mm (2in)

tools and equipment

Chainsaw
Jigsaw

1 The posts for the compost bins are 1300mm (52in) and formed from sleepers cut in half with a chainsaw. (See page 118 for safety notes on using a chainsaw.) You can angle the tops so that they shed rainwater. Dig 400mm (16in) deep holes for the posts and position them with the narrower face to the front. Set them vertically using a spirit-level, and secure them with rammed, backfilled soil.

2 Nail two strips of batten, 850mm (34in) long, to each face of the sleepers that will carry the infill strips, using three 50mm (2in) nails per batten. The distance between the two strips depends on the material you choose to fill the gaps; here a gap of 25mm (1in) is shown to take horizontal log rounds.

Side panels: rustic logs

3 If your logs are of even diameter and will stack regularly on top of each other, you can space the battens accordingly. If not, you will need to shape the ends first. Temporarily hammer two nails into the top of the sleeper to locate the end of the log. Cut the log to fit snugly between the sleepers, then saw about one-third of the way through the log about 25mm (1in) from the end. Turn the log over and repeat on the other side.

4 Chisel out the two pieces of wood, leaving a rectangular tongue in the middle, and space the battens so that the tongue will fit between them.

5 The rustic logs stack neatly on top of one another so that they form one side of the compost bin.

Side panels: bark-clad log strips

6 Shaping the ends is, again, only necessary if your log strips are of uneven thicknesses, otherwise they will stack well on top of one another. Using a chisel, take out the end section of wood, leaving a good 25mm (1in) tongue on the bark side of the strip to slot between the battens.

7 The bark-clad timber stack to form the infill between the posts.

Side panels: wavy boards

8 To allow aeration of the compost, cut out scallop shapes in the edges of the boards with a jigsaw.

9 These boards were tanalized (impregnated with preservative) to prevent them from rotting We also applied a preservative woodstain to give them further protection and for decoration.

plant labels

Many keen gardeners try different ways of labelling their plants, until they discover a system that works for them. Here I have shown six different methods of varying complexity. The printed labels were made using a machine from The Touch Labelling Company. They make a range of machines suitable for use by someone with a small domestic garden, right up to those those used in commerical and public gardens. These provide a uniform, clear, relatively easy-to-make label. The other aluminium label, made by using indented letters from a stamp, is not very easy to read, but has an extremely long lifespan and requires little investment.

Then there are the pale green plastic labels with a hand-written name in a permanent silver paint marker. These markers come in a variety of thicknesses and are available in most office equipment and art shops. The disadvantage is that the plastic labels tend to get displaced, broken or buried over a period of time and need replacing at intervals.

The oak pegs look unobtrusive and are quick and easy to make, but they too need replacing as they slowly rot away. Making the lettering with a pyrograph is fairly quick to do, once you get used to the machine.

Perspex labels are inexpensive to make. These look good in a garden situation – not too obtrusive but clear to read. The labels could be cut to different shapes and made with a small hole so they could be hung from a tree. Using an engraving tool takes a bit of getting used to, and the process can be a little time consuming initially until you get into the swing of it.

Slate is fantastic for labels, but it is costly and rather difficult to engrave, so perhaps it could be reserved only for special plants being given to commemorate a particular occasion – something to be borne in mind!

ROSA PERDITA

ROSA PORTMEIRION

ROSA
GOLDEN CELEBRATION

ROSA MUNDI

ROSA
BARBARA AUSTIN

oak label

We cut out this label from an oak fencing post using a jigsaw, which makes it a simple, inexpensive label. However, the timber will slowly degrade. Having said that, the labels are unobtrusive, will be sympathetic and are easy to make.

MATERIALS oak fencing post; jigsaw, pencil; pyrograph or soldering iron.

1 Mark out the lettering freehand in pencil, in a serif typeface. Give thickness to the lines so that the letters will not be squashed together when burnt in.

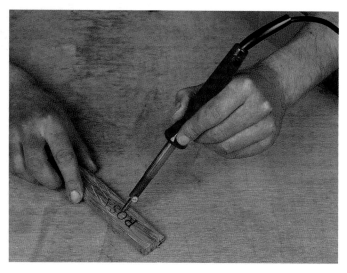

2 Using a pyrograph (purpose-made for the task) or a soldering iron that has a fine tip, burn the lettering into the wood, following the pencil outline.

slate label

This is definitely the most difficult label for an amateur to do well, and it takes time. The finished article is worth the effort for some special plants and will stand the test of time. A stone carver could do the work for you.

MATERIALS slate label; stone carving chisel.

1 Use a stone carving chisel with an angled cutting edge. Scratch the lettering into the slate, using the pointed end for curves and the chisel edge for straight lines. Make repeated light strokes (rather than a few heavy ones).

perspex label

This system is one of my favourites for the amateur gardener. The perspex was cut using a jigsaw and is easy to engrave. The labels look unobtrusive but stylish, fitting in with a modern or traditional garden equally well. The size and shape of the label can be varied and they could be drilled to hang from a branch.

MATERIALS perspex; jigsaw; solvent-based marker pen; electric engraving tool.

1 Mark out the lettering using a solvent-based marker pen. Using an electric engraving tool, go over the letters again and again until you have reached the desired depth. Apply only light pressure.

plastic label

A permanent silver marker pen used on a soft green plastic label gives a combination of colours that is easy to read but not too jarring in a border context. The text is very durable – surprisingly so – and extremely easy to do. The labels will snap if accidentally trodden on.

MATERIALS soft green plastic label; permanent silver marker pen.

1 Ensure that the label is free of grease by washing with liquid detergent, then rinse and allow to dry thoroughly. Shake the silver marker pen before use and apply the lettering freehand, taking care to keep your fingers off the writing surface of the label until dry.

aluminium label with stamped letters

We cut the label from a strip of aluminium from a DIY store using a jigsaw, so the label itself is simple and inexpensive. The lettering is less distinct than the others, but the system is durable and cheap, if a little fiddly.

MATERIALS pencil; aluminium; jigsaw; letter stamps.

1 Mark a pencil base line for the letters as a guide. Using 6mm (¼in) letter stamps, align each stamp with the base line and give it a single sharp blow with the hammer. Work on a solid, non-springy surface.

aluminium labels with self-adhesive letters

This lettering system is used in many gardens with extensive plant collections that are open to the public. The labels should last you a lifetime. We stuck ours on a heavy-duty aluminium label but they will stick to most surfaces. The labels are easy to read and very quick to make.

MATERIALS heavy-duty aluminium; specialist computer.

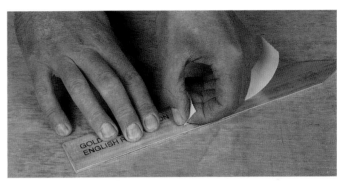

1 The lettering is printed on to a transparent, self-adhesive strip. Peel off about 25mm (1in) of the backing paper and position the strip on the aluminium; press down the end firmly. Peel away the remainder of the backing, pressing down the strip as you go to ensure that no air gets trapped beneath it.

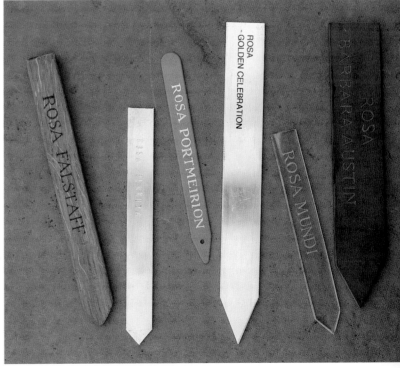

herb cloche

These small timber cloches are extremely useful for over-wintering certain herbs or bringing on some early plants. I use them in the vegetable garden, where they sit in squares of dwarf box hedging, to give me herbs throughout the year. The hedges offer some shelter but they are mainly ornamental, providing extra interest in the winter months. The cloches could look good and be equally useful in the ornamental garden, placed over a plant that has not yet matured enough to be totally hardy in the cold seasons, or popped over some recently planted tender perennials. In this situation they could be painted in a more flamboyant colour, perhaps a strong blue or a mellow yellow.

Because the cloches have been made from softwood, they are lightweight, and in very windy areas it may be necessary to pin them down with a bent wire peg through the frame base. Alternatively, they could be made out of hardwood, which is not a lot more expensive at this size, but it is much more dense and has the added advantage of lasting a good while longer. A drawer knob has been used to form the handle, but this could be replaced by an object with a more exotic shape, such as the onion-shaped finial used for the awning project (see page 108).

MATERIALS

Timber is pressure treated, planed all round/PAR.
Sizes are finished sizes.

Side frames:

  Corner uprights, 4 of 25 x 25 x 330mm
  (1 x 1 x 13in)

  Intermediate uprights, 8 of 20 x 25 x 280mm
  (¾ x 1 x 11in)

  Top and bottom rails: 4 of 25 x 25 x 500mm
  (1 x 1 x 20in)
  4 of 25 x 25 x 550mm (1 x 1 x 22in)

Lid:

  Base frame: 2 of 20 x 25 x 500mm (¾ x 1 x 20in)
  2 of 20 x 25 x 550mm (¾ x 1 x 22in)

  Sloping rails, 4 of 20 x 25 x 522mm (¾ x 1 x 21in)

  Centre block, 20 x 20 x 75mm (¾ x ¾ x 3in)

Glazing, clear acrylic sheet, 2mm (⁵⁄₆₄in) thick (check
dimensions before cutting):

  Side frames, 4 of 500 x 330mm (20 x 13in)

  Lid triangles, 4 of 520mm high x 520mm across
  the base (21 x 21in)

Corner plates, 4 of 50 x 50 x 10mm (2 x 2 x ⅜in),
  and ¾in x No. 6 screws

Finial or drawer knob for lid, approx 30mm (1¼in) dia.

Hook and eye catches for lid, 2 of 30mm (1¼in)

Galvanized metal tent pegs for fixing structure down,
  or galvanized steel rod, 3mm (⅛in) dia., 2 of 230mm
  (9in) long

Panel pins, 40mm (1½in)

Round wire nail, 1 of 40mm (1½in)

Waterproof woodworking adhesive or gap-filling
  adhesive

Clear silicone sealant

tools and equipment

Straightedge

Spirit-based marker pen

Cartridge frame gun (to apply adhesive and sealant)

1 First make up the side frames. These are constructed as 'ladder' sections, with the 'rungs' butt-jointed between the top and bottom rails. Two of the sides are complete rectangles, with corner uprights overlapping the ends of the top and bottom rails. The other two have no ends and are joined to the corner uprights *in situ*.

2 If you want to paint the cloche, do so before glazing it. Glaze the two side frames with no corner uprights in order to keep them rigid. Cut the acrylic sheet to the full size of the frames by first marking with a spirit-based marker pen, then scoring along the marked line against a straight edge. Snap along the line by bending down the sheet over the edge of the workbench. Apply a bead of clear silicone sealant to one face of the frame.

7 The sloping lid rails that form the pyramid are joined at the apex to a short block of timber, 20 x 20mm (¾ x ¾ in) in section. Cut these rails to an overall length of 522mm (21in) and mitre the ends at 45 degrees across the 25mm (1in) wide faces, in opposite directions. Position the lid base with the corner plates downwards, and glue and pin the rails to each corner, sloping up to the apex.

8 Cut the block of wood for the apex to a length of 75mm (3in). On each face of the block, insert a panel pin 40mm (1½ in) from the bottom, to act as a stop for the mitred end of each rail. While another person holds the top assembly, apply gap-filling adhesive to each face of the block and pin each rail through the mitred end to the block. Leave until the adhesive has hardened.

3 Peel off the protective film from the acrylic sheet, then press the cut sheet firmly on to the silicone sealant.

4 Assemble the four side frames on a flat surface by glueing (with woodworking adhesive or gap-filling adhesive) and pinning through the corner uprights into the ends of the top and bottom rails. Measure the distance between the glazed frames and glaze the other two side frames in the same way.

5 Seal the joints at the corners with more sealant to make the cloche draughtproof.

6 Check the outside length of the side frames and cut the four lid base members to match. Two of these should be shorter by twice the timber thickness. Make up the square lid base frame with butt joints as before. Reinforce these joints by screwing a flat, corner plate over each joint, using ¾ in x No. 6 screws.

9 Remove the temporary panel pins and cut off the wood block 6mm (¼ in) above the apex of the sloping rails. Drill a hole into the block to be a tight fit for a 38mm (1½ in) nail. Hammer the nail into the centre of the underside of a wooden drawer knob so that 20mm (¾ in) projects, then cut off the nail head with pliers or a hacksaw. Apply gap-filling adhesive to the top of the block and push in the projecting nail.

10 The lid is glazed from the outside, the angle of the sloping rails providing a back-stop for the glazing panels. Measure the sides of the triangle on the surface and deduct 3mm (⅛ in) from the height and width. Cut the triangular panels to this size. Apply silicone sealant to the lid rails and push the panels into position. Apply more sealant round the outside of the panel.

11 To secure the lid to the base we fitted a hook and eye on each side. Screw in the eyes first, in the centre of each top rail, then fit each hook through the eye. Press down the lid firmly, to ensure that it will be a tight fit, and screw the hook to the lid.

12 For extremely windy conditions, the cloche is secured to the ground with a metal tent peg on each side. Drill through the centre of each bottom rail to take the peg. If you are making these yourself, use a 230mm (9in) length of 3mm (⅛in) diameter galvanized steel rod. Bend 25mm (1in) at one end through about 90 degrees.

timber and steel planter

This is a traditional planter design, but I have adapted it by putting in galvanized steel panels to give it a more up-to-date look. These containers are relatively large (approximately 500 x 500 x 500mm/20 x 20 x 20in), but obviously the design can be scaled up or down to fit into your surroundings. If you are going to plant them out with large, heavy specimens then it will be necessary to support the galvanized base on the underside. I do this by placing a 25mm (1in) thick log-round underneath, which is wide enough to support the base but not wide enough to show, and then I put the drainage holes around the edge of this.

The timber work is fairly straightforward and should be constructed first to give the dimensions for the container. Bending the metal sheet is more difficult. Metal workers will supply the sheet cut to size to fit within your timber work, and if you want to simplify the DIY side you could probably also have the sheets shaped at the same time.

The shape of the finials could be altered to an oval, onion or pyramid if preferred. Also, the timber could be stained if you want a brighter finish; blue would work particularly well with the silver. The shape need not be square – a trough design would work well. If you are not a fan of the contemporary look, you could infill the sides with plywood and paint all the woodwork with an opaque woodstain.

MATERIALS

All timber for the posts and rails is pressure treated, prepared (PAR). Sizes are finished sizes.

Corner posts, 4 of 50 x 50 x 580mm
(2 x 2 x 23in)

Top and bottom rails:
4 of 50 x 50 x 500mm
(2 x 2 x 20in)
4 of 50 x 50 x 460mm
(2 x 2 x 18½ in)

Galvanized steel sheet:
1 of 1400 x 400 x 0.5mm
(56 x 16 x ⅟₅₀ in)
2 of 550 x 440 x 0.5mm
(22 x 17½ x ⅟₅₀ in)

Timber ball finials, 4 of 65mm
(2½ in) dia.

Dowel, 6mm (¼ in) dia., 100mm
(4in) long

Angle brackets, steel, 8 of 65 x 65
x 18mm (2½ x 2½ x ¾ in)

Screws, 1in x No. 8

Gap-filling adhesive mastic

Timber offcuts:
2 of 25 x 50 x 600mm
(1 x 2 x 24in) approx
1 of 50 x 75 x 450mm
(2 x 3 x 18in) approx

tools and equipment

Tenon saw

High speed steel (HSS) twist drill bits, 3 and 6mm (⅛ and ¼ in) dia.

Mallet

Ear defenders

Cartridge frame gun

The timber framework is made from posts and rails joined with halving joints. The galvanized container is in three parts. The bottom and two opposite sides are formed from the longer sheet as a flat-bottomed U-shape. The other two panels are identical to each other and run from top to bottom on opposite sides; the vertical edges and the bottom edge are bent through 90 degrees and fit inside the U. Measure up the metal panels to fit inside the timber framework, allowing for the angle brackets which are about 1.5mm (⅟₁₆ in) thick. The panels should finish 5mm (¼ in) below the top edge of the top rails and flush with the underside of the bottom rails. The dimensions for the metal sheet (below) are for guidance only and will depend on the section of the timber. You should wear ear defenders when hammering the metal.

1 Mark out halving joints in the corner posts and the top and bottom rails: the posts project 50mm (2in) above the top rails and 25mm (1in) below the bottom rails, and the front and back rails overlap the ends of the side rails at the corners. Mark the joints slightly deeper in the rails than in the posts so as not to weaken the latter. Cut down the sides of the joints with a tenon saw, and chisel out the waste.

2 Apply adhesive to all the joint surfaces then join the rails to the posts by screwing an angle bracket to the rails on the inside of each corner, at top and bottom.

3 Chamfer the top edges of each corner post using a sharp block plane or a planer file, working from the corners towards the centre of each edge to avoid splitting the corners. Drill 12mm (½ in) into the top of each post to take a 6mm (¼ in) dowel for attaching the finial, and drill a corresponding hole in each finial.

4 Form the flat-bottomed U-shape, with sides 500mm (20in) and base 400mm (16in). Clamp the sheet to the bench, with the bend position above the edge of the bench and a batten on top of it, and make the initial stages of the bend by hand. Then, when the angle is nearly 90 degrees, hammer backwards and forwards along the bend to make a sharp angle.

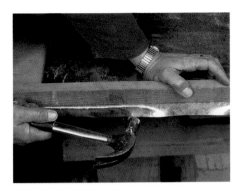

5 Bend the long edges of the two small steel sheets to fit inside the U by clamping them between two battens, 20mm (³⁄₄ in) from the edge. You can use two bolts (as we did) or a pair of G-clamps. Then position the lower batten against the edge of your workbench and gradually hammer down the projecting edge, starting at one end and working backwards and forwards along it, until it is at 90 degrees to the surface.

6 Cut a slot in the bent edges of each side panel, 500mm (20in) down from the top, to enable the bottom edge to be bent up. Bend in the 50mm (2in) end section of the panel edges slightly so that they will fit inside the vertical edges when the bottom is bent up.

7 Cut a piece of 50 x 75mm (2 x 3in) timber to fit exactly between the bent edges and clamp the side panel over the 50mm (2in) face of the timber, aligning the slots with the edge of the timber. Crease down a 50mm (2in) flange, working to and fro with a hammer. When you have bent it through 90 degrees, turn over the panel and hammer out any dents in the edge from the inside.

8 Insert the U-shaped panel into the framework, flush with the underside of the bottom rails, then insert the individual side panels – they should fit snuggly inside the U and be level at the top. Drill two 3mm (¹⁄₈ in) diameter holes through the top edge of each panel, 90mm (3¹⁄₂ in) in from the corners.

9 Secure the panels to the top rails of the framework with 1in x No. 8 screws. Drill six 6mm (¹⁄₄ in) drainage holes in the base of the container, widely spaced so as not to weaken the metal.

10 Insert a 25mm (1in) length of dowel in each finial, apply gap-filling adhesive to the top of the posts and tap the finials firmly on to the post tops with a mallet. Remove excess adhesive with the point of a nail.

timber balustrade

If you have always hankered after the classical touch but were not sure how to accommodate it, you could consider constructing this balustrade fencing. It is one of the simpler projects and requires little skill and finance. The archway is designed to frame a entrance way into another part of the garden. I have also used it very successfully in slightly different circumstances; once to frame a view on top of a retaining wall. I then adapted the design by continuing the 'balustrading' all the way along the bottom. Another way I have used it is against a blank, rendered wall and then a trompe l'oeil was painted in the archway. In that case I bolted the fencing to the wall and did not run the posts into the ground.

The fake balustrades are cut out of plywood, and as such are two dimensional. If you want to enhance the illusion, you can paint the horizontal lines shown on the diagram on page 42 and the shadow on one side of the 'bottles' (shapes at the bottom) using a similar approach to the way the shadow was painted on the trompe l'oeil arbour (see page 55). However, this will only work well if you put it in a shady place so that real shadows do not fall in the opposite direction, causing visual confusion!

MATERIALS

All timber is sawn, pressure treated. Sizes are actual.

Posts:
  2 of 100 x 100 x 2300mm (4 x 4 x 92in)
  2 of 100 x 100 x 2700mm (4 x 4 x 108in)

Arches (see diagram): marine plywood, 1 sheet, 2440 x 1220 x 25mm (96 x 48 x 1in)

Bottles (see diagram): marine plywood, 1 sheet, 2440 x 1220 x 18mm (96 x 48 x ¾ in) *See below*

Back rails, 4 of 50 x 75 x 1000mm (2 x 3 x 40in)

Capping strips, 2 of 25 x 38 x 1075mm (1 x 1½ x 43in)

Oval finials with plinth, 4 of 75mm (3in) dia.

Woodstain

Screws, 2 and 3in x No. 8

Panel pins, 40mm (1½ in)

Thin cardboard for bottle template, 800 x 300mm (32 x 12in) approx

tools and equipment
Jigsaw
Circular saw
Smoothing plane

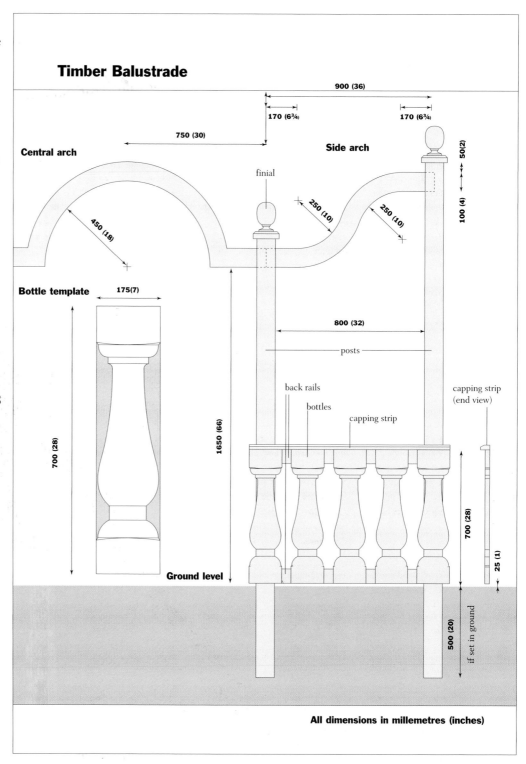

Timber Balustrade

Central arch

Side arch

900 (36)

170 (6¾)   170 (6¾)

750 (30)

finial

50(2)

100 (4)

450 (18)

250 (10)   250 (10)

Bottle template   175(7)

800 (32)

posts

700 (28)

1650 (66)

back rails

bottles

capping strip

capping strip (end view)

700 (28)

25 (1)

Ground level

500 (20)

if set in ground

All dimensions in millemetres (inches)

It is possible to get away with just one sheet of 25mm (1in) plywood, but the bottles are more difficult to cut out of the greater thickness.

1 Mark out the central arch on 25mm (1in) plywood to the dimensions shown in the diagram. Use a beam compass made from a length of batten with a nail through one end. Cut out the arch with a jigsaw. Make the two outer arches in the same way.

2 Enlarge the bottle template to actual size and stick it on to thin card; cut out a template. Tape the template on to 18mm (¾ in) plywood and mark round it. Cut out the shape with a jigsaw, cutting from both directions into the angles. You will need ten bottles in all.

3 Mark a halving joint on both ends of the back rails to half the thickness and as long as the width of the post. Clamp the rail in a vice and make a series of cuts, every 6mm (¼ in), down to the base line using a circular saw set to this depth.

4 Remove the waste with a sharp bevel-edged chisel, working from the end of the rail and with the bevelled face upwards.

5 Lay the back rail across the post and mark the width of the rail on the post. Measure the remaining thickness of timber in the joint and mark the depth line for the joint on the post at this distance down from the surface.

6 Make a series of cuts across the post down to the depth line (as in stage 3) and chisel out the waste, this time working from both sides of the post towards the centre. Test fit the back rail and adjust the joint as necessary by shaving off small slivers with the chisel.

7 Attach the back rails to the post with two 2in x No. 8 screws at each end, on the diagonal of the joint.

8 Centre the outer bottles over the posts and set the other three bottles, equally spaced, between them. Screw them to the back rails with two 2in x No. 8 screws at each end.

9 The arches are screwed to the opposite face of the posts. The half arches fit in a closed recess in the outer posts: make a series of cuts down to the base line from the edge, then chisel out the waste. The arches meet at the centre of the inner posts.

10 Cut the capping strip to length, so as to completely cover the bottles, and plane a chamfer on the front top edge. Screw the capping strip to the posts with two 3in x No. 8 screws at each end.

11 Fit an oval finial to each post top by pinning through the plinth; blunt the end of the 40mm (1½in) panel pins first to avoid splitting the wood. When the balustrade is installed, the bottles should be 25mm (1in) above ground.

12 Slightly round off any sharp corners and edges with a plane – both at body and head height – before applying your chosen finish. We used Jotun's Demidekk colour BS12821.

trompe l'oeil doors

A simple way to make a contained garden look as though it leads on to somewhere else is to put an entrance way at the end of it. These doors are designed to fix on to a wall or fence to create the illusion of something happening beyond. They can also be useful for screening an unsightly object on the other side of the garden boundary, as they are higher than the standard 1.8m (6ft) fence.

The style of the doors can vary in many ways. An ogee arch has been selected, which may look a little over-the-top in some gardens, where a Roman or triangular arch might be more suitable. The colour blue, painted with an opaque woodstain, also stands out dramatically, but for a less strident effect, you could use a calmer olive green. The thin plywood panels behind the windows are painted dark grey to look like glass. As an alternative to plywood, you could fit acrylic mirrors, to fool the eye into thinking that your garden carries on over the other side; the close trellis prevents you from seeing too much – which would give the game away too soon.

The doors are surrounded by trellis made from roofing battens, and sit flush with the front of the trellis. The overall size of our trellis is 1830mm wide by 2440mm high (72 x 96in). By screwing three of the horizontal trellis battens to the back of the doors, they can be used to mount the doors on the wall or fence and avoid the need to drill holes through the painted surface.

There is a lot of scope for playing with the details in this project. Real metal hinges and knobs could be used if you wanted it to look more authentic, or if you are not over-confident with your painting skills. A simple wooden picket gate topped by a plywood arch in front of a mirror, would – in a shady place – really lead you to believe that your space continued further afield.

MATERIALS

Marine plywood, 1 sheet
2440 x 1220 x 18mm (96 x
48 x ¾ in)

Marine plywood, 1 sheet
1000 x 1000 x 6mm (40 x
40 x ¼in)

Cast acrylic sheet with mirror finish
(optional), 1000 x 900 x 3mm
(40 x 36 x ⅛ in) approx.

Outer trellis: timber roofing
batten, 19 x 38 x 36m
(¾ x 1½ in x 120ft) approx

Window trellis: pressure-
treated planed timber
batten (PAR), 9 x 22mm x 10m
(⅜ x ⅞in x 34ft)

Opaque woodstain, light blue
(Jotun's Demidekk), also white,
dark blue, grey and violet

Acrylic paints, raw sienna,
cadmium yellow, green,
raw umber and white

Black marker pen

Panel pins, 18 and 40mm
(¾ and 1½in)

Screws, 2in x No. 8

Masonry nails, 50mm (2in)
(for fixing trellis to wall)

Oval nails, 40mm (1½in)

Wall plugs

tools and equipment

Jigsaw, variable speed, with
medium blade/timber
and fine blade/plastics

Paintbrushes, 12, 25 and 50mm
(½, 1 and 2in)

Artist's brush, size 4

Safety goggles (if using masonry nails)

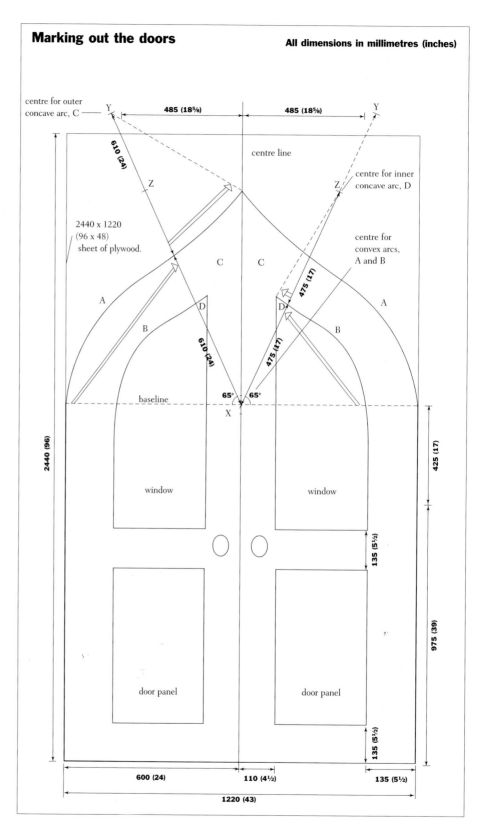

Marking out the doors   **All dimensions in millimetres (inches)**

MAKING THE DOORS

1 Draw the straight lines of the door panels and windows on to a 2440 x 1220mm (96 x 48in) sheet of plywood, to the dimensions shown in Marking out the doors (left).

2 Draw the horizontal base line for the arcs.

3 Extend the vertical centre line to the top of the board and make a mark 485mm (18⅝in) each side of it on the top edge.

4 Join these marks to the centre of the base line (X) to form the 65-degree angles.

5 Make a beam compass from a 750mm (30in) length of batten. Drill a clearance hole for a 50mm (2in) nail, 50mm (2in) from one end. Drill two holes to take a pencil, centred 475 and 610mm (17 and 24in) away from it.

6 With the nail on the centre of the baseline (X), mark two convex arcs (A and B), from the base line to the 65-degree angle line, on each side of the centre line.

7 Tape a 200 x 100mm (8 x 4in) offcut of plywood above one top corner of the board and extend the angled line across it. With the nail at centre Y on this line, mark a concave arc (C), from the angled line to the centre line. Repeat on the opposite side.

8 With the nail at centre Z on the angled lines, mark two concave arcs (D), from the angled lines to the edge of the windows.

9 Cut out the outer curves and the windows with a jigsaw. Drill a starting hole for the jigsaw blade at the bottom two corners of the windows, within the marked lines, and cut into the corners from both directions to leave a sharp angle.

10 Cut out the window backing panels from 6mm (¼in) ply, 25mm (1in) larger all round than the openings. Paint them with grey woodstain and pin them in position.

1 We painted the doors all over with light blue opaque woodstain. To create the door panels, paint in two edges as white keylines, then pick out the shadows in dark blue with a little violet added. Alongside the shadows, paint in highlights in white, following the pencil lines freehand.

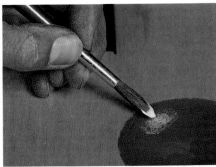

2 Next paint in the door knobs below the right-angled corners of the windows. These are about 75mm (3in) in diameter. We used acrylic paints for this: raw sienna for the brass background colour, then cadmium yellow, green and raw umber for the dark areas. The reflected highlight is again white.

3 The shadows under the knobs are elliptical in shape, with broken edges. The shadow from the boss of the knob tapers inwards as it gets further away from the knob. A fine white keyline separates the knob from its shadow.

4 The dividing line between the two doors was formed with a black marker pen against a straightedge. Alongside the black line is a white keyline which is broken where it crosses the shadow of the knob.

5 Make the trellis for the windows by first cutting the horizontal strips and positioning them in the opening. Then mark and cut the vertical strips and pin them to the horizontals. We made a spacer block for these: the width is equal to the width of the window minus the width of four battens, divided by five.

INSTALLING THE DOORS

Screw three full length trellis battens to the back of the doors: one above and one below the window panels; and one along the bottom edge. Work out the exact position of these battens to tie in with the overall trellis pattern. Stand the doors in position and screw the battens to the wall or fence.

Cut the remaining horizontal battens to tuck behind the edge of the doors, and fix them to the background with nails or masonry nails. Pre-drill the battens for masonry nails and wear safety goggles when hammering them. Cut the vertical battens to but up to the edge of the doors and nail them to the horizontals with 40mm (1½in) oval nails.

false stone window

This project has a theatrical bent – utilizing a piece of vacuum-formed ABS moulding in the form of a window, to add a quirky look to a high wall. With a little practice in paint effects, it will be fairly easy to transform the window into something extremely convincing. Various grades of moulded material are available, some less substantial (and more costly) than the one we have used here, which should still last for a good while if treated with respect.

We used woodstain on the plywood background in a range of olive greens that we then diluted down with white to create the lighter green for the trellis. The plywood background could be treated with a paint effect to give the illusion of stone blocking, or else a drab, dark green paint finish could be almost smothered with a climbing plant.

Clever siting of the 'window' will make all the difference: tucked in the back of a shady border against a hedge it will be very convincing, but if sited too close to a path more inquisitive people might be tempted to inspect it more closely and tap it!

There are many different types of architectural features available in vacuum-formed mouldings. The supplier stocks all manner of columns, friezes and balustrades in a huge range of sizes and styles. If you want to go overboard in your garden and add a theatrical touch, then this is an inexpensive and fun source to think about.

MATERIALS

Vacuum-formed Gothic window

Expanding foam filler, 1 large can

Cast acrylic sheet with a mirror
    finish, 800 x 1000 x 3mm
    (32 x 40 x ⅛ in) approx

Marine plywood backing board,
    1220 x 1830 x 18mm
    (48 x 72 x ¾ in)

Roofing battens for trellis
    surround, 19 x 38mm (¾ x
    1½ in) x 26m (85ft) approx

Cellulose car body spray paints:
    grey primer, black and yellow

Acrylic paints: green and yellow
    ochre

Woodstain: dark olive green, white

Impact adhesive

Screws, 1½in x No. 8

Black mastic

Oval nails, 38mm (1½in)

tools and equipment

Circular saw or jigsaw (optional)

Metal straightedge

Spirit-based marker pen

Respirator mask

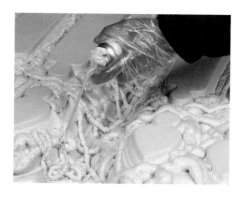

1 The window moulding that we used was not the thinnest grade available, and was quite rigid and resilient to knocks. Even so, we firmed it up by injecting it with expanding polyurethane foam filler. A light spray of water beforehand helps its adherence. Wear the gloves supplied with the filler as it is difficult to remove from your hands. Nail-varnish remover will enable you to clear the applicator tube after use.

2 When the filler has set hard, turn over the moulding (face upwards) on to a flat surface on which you can cut, and cut out the recessed panels with a sharp handyman's knife. Change the blade frequently to avoid tearing the plastic. Clean up any rough edges.

3 Spray the moulding with three colours of cellulose car body paint – black, yellow and grey primer – so that they merge in together. The cellulose paint gives a matt surface to the shiny plastic and acts as a good base for the following treatment. (Wear a respirator mask when using spray paint.)

4 Now, using acrylic paints in green and yellow ochre, brush on the effect of algae to the mock stonework. The underlying grey and yellow shows the finished effect of the spray treatment.

5 Next, cut the mirror to size. If the cut-out areas of the moulding are level with the surrounding flat border, cut the mirror to the total size of the moulding. If the cut-outs are slightly raised above the border, you have two options: either cut the mirror to fit inside the border; or cut individual rectangles to fit behind the cut-outs.

Mark the size for the mirror on the protective film using a spirit-based marker pen, then, with the handyman's knife, score along the cutting line several times against a straightedge, using repeated light strokes rather than a few heavy ones and ensuring that the cuts reach right to the edges. It is important that each score line follows the same route: if any veer away from the marked line, you may end up with a jagged edge (although this will be covered over later).

6 Turn the mirror over, and measure and mark the position of the cutting line on the back surface. Clamp a batten along this line and place a board beneath it, then, with a person at each end of the board, pull it up to bend back the mirror, which should snap off cleanly.

Stick the mirror to the plywood backing board with impact adhesive, applied in matching bands to the back of the mirror and the plywood. When the adhesive is touch dry (see instructions on the container), position one edge of the mirror on the plywood, curve the centre towards the board slightly, and carefully lower it into position, pressing it down firmly as you progress.

7 Check that no foam projects beyond the back of the window moulding, and remove any that does with a handsaw so that it will lie flat on the mirror. Remove the protective film from the front of the mirror and place the window in position on it. Make up the surrounding trellis from the roofing batten joined with oval nails, so that the central hole fits round the moulding and the inner trellis laths sit over the flange that surrounds the window. Lower the trellis on to the moulding. Choosing positions where the screws will be least obvious, drill pilot holes through the trellis, the flange and the mirror into the plywood.

8 Screw the trellis in place with 1½ in x No. 8 screws. Touch over the screwheads with the same paint as used on the trellis. When the moulding is secured, seal the edges of the window openings to the mirror with black mastic and smooth it with a wet finger.

trompe l'oeil arbour

This arbour is purely an illusion, giving the effect of an intricate structure over a bench. It is formed from plywood sheets cut to the pattern shown on page 56. The pattern can be drawn out or enlarged on the large photocopying machines that are available in some large architects' offices or printing shops. I enlarged one half of the design (which the machine did on two pieces of paper, and which I then stuck together). After marking and cutting out the first half of the arbour, I used the cut-out trellis as a template to mark the second half, and turned over the photocopy enlargement of the base details and used it as a mirror image.

Although the project looks tricky, the most difficult part is cutting out the plywood with a jigsaw. A variable-speed machine will enable you to slow right down for the awkward parts and to get a good accurate finish. The paint effects are fairly simple, and if you go wrong, you can simply paint over it again to put it right.

This sort of structure fits into a range of settings, both modern and old. A strident blue paint colour (as shown in the photograph) gives it a contemporary look, while dark green can make it look more traditional. The seat design can also swing the effect to the old or new: we used a reconstituted stone seat which was specially made for me. The arbour can be screwed to a wall, or mounted in the open on posts set into post sockets, as shown here.

It would be possible to put mirror behind the 'trellis' part of the arbour, instead of hedging as we have used here. But this would work best in a very shady situation or else the mirror could work against the three-dimensional effect of the trellis.

Using trellis with mirrors to provide an illusion of depth is very versatile: you could design a tunnel effect or an alcove with a small window at the top.

MATERIALS

Marine plywood, 3 sheets, 2440 x 1220 x 12mm
   (96 x 48 x ½ in)

Cast acrylic sheet with mirror finish (optional), 1 sheet,
   2440 x 1220 x 3mm (96 x 48 x ⅛in)

Screws, 1in x No. 8

Masking tape

Spray adhesive

Black spray paint

Opaque woodstain: light blue, black, dark green
   and white

Glass paint, olive green (optional)

For installing the arbour:

Wall fixing:

   Screws, 2½in x No. 8

   Wall plugs

   Round wire nails, 2 of 100mm (4in)

Post fixing:

   Fence posts, 2 of 75 x 75mm (3 x 3in):

      with no mirror, 600mm (24in) long;

      with mirror, 1200mm (48in) long

   Cross rail, 75 x 75x 1220mm (3 x 3 x 48in)

   Post sockets, 2 of 75 x 75 x 600mm (3 x 3 x 24in)

   Screws, 2½in x No. 8

tools and equipment

Jigsaw, variable speed, with medium blade for timber
   and very fine-toothed blade for plastics (optional)

Scalpel or sharp craft knife

Straightedge

Spirit-based marker pen

Paintbrushes, 12, 25 and 50mm (½, 1 and 2in)

Artist's brush, size 4

Respirator mask

Marking out the design

The arbour is made in two halves, and is cut from two sheets of plywood joined at the long edges. Cut these to a length of 1840mm (72¾ in) and keep the offcuts for later use. Enlarge half the template on page 56–57 in sections to an overall width of 1220mm (48in). Stick the sheets together with masking tape and cut round the outline. Spray adhesive all over the back of the enlarged template, allow it to become touch dry, and stick the template to one sheet of plywood with the centre edge against the long edge of the ply and the bottom edges flush. Press it down firmly.

    Cut out the holes in the trellis on the template with a sharp craft knife and remove them, leaving the black lines in place; it doesn't matter if you cut into the plywood. Change the blade frequently to avoid tearing the paper. On the lower part of the template – the plinth areas and the curved back – cut out dashed lines instead, to a width of about 3mm (⅛ in), to make a stencil for the base details.

1 Spray over the cut-out areas and round the outline with black paint. When the paint has dried, peel off the template: you will be left with cutting lines for the trellis and dashed detail lines of the base; join up the dashes freehand. Drill a starting hole for the jigsaw in each trellis panel and cut them out, working from both directions into the angles.

2 We painted the arbour all over with blue woodstain, taking care to leave the base detail lines visible. We lightened the 'horizontal' surface of the base section with white. Depict the curved vertical panel with gradated white shading, using vertical strokes of the 25mm (1in) paintbrush. Pick out highlights at the top corner in white, using the artist's brush.

3 The ground below the base panel, which will appear behind the stone seat, is a semi-elliptical area of dark green to the bottom of the plywood, to represent grass. Hold the brush at 90 degrees to the line of the ellipse and paint away from the edge.

4 Paint in the shadow that the arbour would form on the curved base and on the ground in dark blue, formed by mixing in some black. You will need both halves of the arbour positioned together for this. Where the shadow meets the curved panel, make short, light strokes with the brush to leave a dappled, broken edge to the shadow.

5 Form the 'recessed' plinth panels by applying a dark blue shadow to the top edge and one side, and white highlights to the other two edges, using an artist's brush. Join the two arbour halves together at the bottom using the two 600mm (24in) wide offcuts of plywood. Screw one strip centrally across the join, flush with the bottom edge. Screw the two halves of the other strip each side of it.

6 Paint in the shadow detail on the trellis using the photograph on page 53 as a guide. The edge of the shadow forms a curved line on the trellis, and in this case it would have quite a hard edge because it is close to the point of origin.

 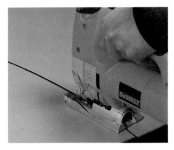  

7 If you wish to put acrylic mirror on the back this is the procedure: lay the mirror flat, with the back surface uppermost, and place the arbour on top of it with the plywood offcuts butting up to the long edge. Mark round the plywood on to the mirror with a spirit-based marker pen.

8 Cut the mirror to shape with a very fine-toothed blade in a jigsaw. Ensure that the mirror is flat and is well supported next to the cut. Set the jigsaw to slow speed and cut with only slight forward pressure. Any straight cuts can be made using the technique described for the False Stone Window on page 51.

9 Lay the mirror, with the protective film uppermost, on the remaining sheet of plywood, flush at the bottom edge. This will be fixed as a backing to the mirror and will also join together the two halves of the arbour above the seat. Mark round the mirror and cut the plywood to shape.

10 Peel off the protective film from the mirror and lay the arbour trellis over it. Paint the shadow areas on the mirror using an olive green (chartreuse) glass paint. Finally, sandwich the mirror between the arbour and the backing panel, drill pilot holes through the plywood and mirror at 230mm (9in) intervals round the edge and up both sides of the centre vertical, and screw the layers together from the back using 1in x No. 8 screws.

INSTALLING THE ARBOUR

Wall fixing

Position the arbour against the wall and drill clearance holes for No. 8 screws through it into the wall to mark the fixing positions: two near the top, two half way up and two near the bottom. Drill and plug the wall and countersink the holes in the plywood so that the screwheads will lie flush. Screw the arbour to the wall with 2½ in x No. 8 screws and touch over the screwheads with a matching colour.

Post fixing

Hold the arbour in position and mark the post positions on the ground, 610mm (24in) in from each edge. Knock in two post sockets at these positions (making sure that the clamping screws face backwards), insert the posts and tighten the securing screws. Screw the cross rail on top of the two posts through counterbored holes. Place the arbour in position again and secure it to the posts and rail with six screws (for short posts) or eight screws (for long posts).

Caution: Post socket spikes penetrate 600mm (24in) into the ground. Do not insert them in the vicinity of underground services. If in any doubt, contact your service provider(s) first.

All dimensions in millimetres (inches)

Template for Trompe l'Oeil Arbour

2440 (96)

shell wall fountain

A shell-covered mask that dribbles water into a small pool or pebble feature is a simple way to add water in a garden. This easy, though time-consuming, project utilizes shells, pebbles, sand and water – which all work comfortably together. The mask design has been kept quite basic, but you may decide when you see the vast range of shells that is available that you want to go to town and create a more intricate affair. Instead of filling the gaps between the shells with sand you could overlap the shells slightly which gives a better finished product, but takes a little more time and practice.

The pebble feature in the base has been made slightly more detailed by adding the paler pebbles in a spiral directly on to the darker pebbles. Alternatively, a pattern worked of larger shells, a large codestone ammonite, or some gold-painted pebbles in a circle near the top would add a different twist.

The planting around a feature like this contributes greatly to the overall effect. By using bold, large-leafed marginal plants, such as *Gunnera manicata*, we have emphasized the aquatic feel. If your soil is dry, like mine, you can still plant moisture lovers, but you need to make a mini bog garden to sustain them. This is created by digging a large hole about 600mm (24in) deep and lining it with a heavy-duty butyl or polythene liner with a few holes punched in it. Backfill the lined hole and plant as normal. The liner reduces the drainage of the area, and the holes allow some drainage so the water does not become stagnant.

PLEASE NOTE:
The black cable visible on the wall in some of the photographs on pages 60 to 62 is a 12-volt supply cable to our garden lights. NEVER RUN A MAINS-VOLTAGE CABLE IN THIS MANNER.

MATERIALS

Marine plywood, 18mm (¾in) thick, approx 400 x 500mm (16 x 20in)

Shells (four types used):

  Pecten pallium, approx 30 of 50-65mm (2-2½ in)

  Pecten senatorius, approx 10 of 65-75mm (2½ -3in)

  Mussels, approx 40

  Scallop, 1

Cobbles, approx 150 of 50-150mm (2-6in)

Submersible pump, low-voltage (24V), capable of 2750 lit/hr (600 gal/hr)

  (*The pump should be fitted with a floation switch or thermal cut-out for protection if the water level falls below the inlet*)

Large waterproof container, eg dustbin cut down in height

High-tensile welded and galvanized steel mesh, 50mm (2in) mesh size, 300mm (12in) larger in both directions than container

Butyl liner, 2 x 3m (6ft 6in x 10ft)

Reinforced hose pipe, 17mm (1¹⁄₁₆ in) dia.; to determine length, see steps 5 and 12

Copper pipe, 15mm (½ in) dia. x 150mm (6in)

Gap-filling adhesive mastic

PVA adhesive

Sand, kiln-dried, silver (to fill gaps between shells)

Grey opaque woodstain or similar

tools and equipment

Heavy-duty electric drill (500W minimum)

Long masonry bit and extension sleeve (depending on wall thickness), 19mm (¾in) dia.

Bolt cutters or heavy-duty pliers with wire-cutter

Jigsaw

Spray marker

Cartridge frame gun

Flat file

Safety goggles and dust mask

Thick gauntlets or gloves

1 Mark out a semi-circle for the pool on the soil, using white spray marker paint. The area should be large enough to incorporate a reservoir for the pump, and we also planned to have a bog margin at both sides. Carefully dig round just inside the line so as to leave the line standing.

2 Excavate from the edge inwards at a gentle slope downwards towards the centre, starting at ground level at the perimeter. A gradient of about 1 in 4 is suitable.

3 Make the tank for the water from a plastic dustbin with the rim cut off; you can use a handsaw for this. Position the tank centrally in the hole and backfill round it with soil, firming it down as you fill.

4 At the surface, firm the soil down round the top of the tank and smooth the surrounding area to a dished shape, so that water will run down to the centre. Remove any soil from inside the tank. Place three or four large cobbles in the base of the tank on which to stand the pump, to prevent the inlet from becoming choked up with sediment.

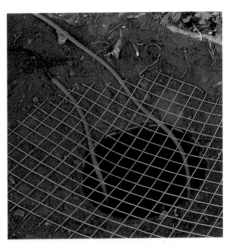

5 Stand the pump on the cobbles and make sure that it is stable, then run the power lead and outlet hose up to the surface. The hose must be long enough to go through the wall, up the back of the wall and through the wall again to the back of the mask fountain. The power lead is pre-fitted and should be connected to the power supply when the rest of the installation is completed.

6 The cobbles above the tank are supported on welded and galvanized high-tensile steel mesh. Using the cut-off rim of the bin as a guide, cut a square of mesh at least 150mm (6in) larger all round than the tank using pliers or bolt-cutters. Wear thick gloves and safety goggles when doing this. Bend the centre of the mesh inwards to a slightly dished shape.

7 Sleeve the power lead from the pump in a length of hose by slitting along the wall of the hose. Arrange the outlet hose and the power lead so that they run towards their destinations and place the mesh centrally over the tank, dish downwards, making sure it is well supported.

8 Cut a piece of heavy-duty butyl rubber pond liner to cover the entire area with 300mm (12in) extra all round. Position it centrally over the excavation and remove wrinkles as far as possible.

9 In the centre of the liner – making sure this is over the centre of the tank – cut a 100mm (4in) square hole. This allows the water from the fountain to return through the cobbles to the tank.

10 Place cobbles on the liner, starting with the large ones and covering any gaps with smaller cobble stones. They should conceal the liner completely.

11 Where the outlet hose is to run through the wall, drill a hole using a long masonry bit. If you are drilling through a 230mm (9in) brick wall, you should be able to hire or buy a single drill bit for the job. For thicker walls you willl need a bit with a threaded shank, and an extension sleeve into which this fits. Withdraw the bit from the hole frequently to allow it to cool and to clear dust from the spiral.

12 Feed the hose through the wall and ensure that there is sufficient length to reach up the back of the wall to where the mask fountain will be and to pass through the wall again, leaving about 300mm (12in) spare to help during installation. Build up the cobbles round the exposed hose to conceal it.

13 Drill another hole through the wall (as in stage 11) to take the hose to the back of the mask and feed the hose through the hole. Ensure that the hose does not kink where it changes direction, by bending it through gentle curves.

14 Cut out the baseboard for the mask in the shape of a flatfish, to an overall size of 400mm long by 300mm wide (16 x 12in) from marine plywood. Paint the board with opaque woodstain, following the manufacturer's instructions, and allow it to dry. Drill a 15mm (⅝in) diameter hole through the board for the spout, three quarters of the way down from the top.

15 Cut a 150mm (6in) length of 15mm (½in) diameter copper pipe and fit it temporarily in the drilled hole. Set out a design of shells on front of the mask, bedding them into a gap-filling adhesive applied from a cartridge. We placed a scallop shell at the top and then laid a border of *Pecten pallium*. The eyes, nose and mouth are *Pecten senatorius*.

16 The gaps between the shells are filled with sand. Brush PVA adhesive on to the visible areas of baseboard.

17 Sprinkle kiln-dried soft building sand on to the adhesive. The sand must be dry for it to adhere properly.

18 Halfway up the mask, drill two holes for No. 8 screws where there is a space between the shells.

19 File off any burr from the end of the copper pipe and push one end into the end of the projecting hose from the back of the wall.

20 Insert the pipe through the hole in the mask and hold the mask in position against the wall. Drill through the two screw holes to mark the fixing positions on the wall, then remove the mask and drill and plug the wall to take 2½ in x No. 8 screws (or 4in if there is greenery on the wall).

    If the wall is covered in ivy, like ours is, the marked holes on the wall are hard to find. After marking each one, push a length of rod through the mask before removing it, then pull off the mask while holding the rod in position. That way the marked drilling position will be easy to find.

21 Secure the mask to the wall with screws of the appropriate length. Longer screws help in positioning them when the wall is overgrown. Use a similar technique when drilling, by inserting a length of rod into one of the plugs while fitting the first screw, then remove the rod to fit the second one.

22 When the rest of the construction was completed, we laid a spiral of light-coloured cobbles in the centre of the area which show up well when the darker, background cobbles are wet. The shape of the water jet coming out of the fountain can be adjusted by bending the end of the copper tube – a horizontally-flattened end will produce a fan shape.

sundial

A bare wall or building can be enhanced by a wall-mounted sundial that not only looks good but has a purpose too. We have designed this for a south-facing wall, which is at 51 degrees latitude in the northern hemisphere. If your wall or fence is in any other position, you will need to consult a specialist book or contact a specialist society for further information (see page 157). Don't forget that because of the changing aspect of the earth in relation to the sun, the accuracy of the sundial will vary slightly throughout the year.

The sun plaque is made from ABS plastic, which is fairly rigid and tough for this purpose. The design of the board, the choice of colours and words can obviously all be varied to suit the setting.

The project is straightforward, the most difficult element being the bending and cutting of the brass strip, which could probably be undertaken by a local blacksmith or metal worker if you are not willing to try it yourself.

You might like to try an alternative horizontal sundial design that is a favourite with children. It involves marking out a large circle on the ground from a central paving slab where you stand to perform the function of the gnomon (and throw a shadow on to the sundial). Mark the 12 noon line to true north, and position paving to represent the hours all around the edge.

MATERIALS

Sun face in ABS plastic

Marine plywood, 18 x 900 x 950mm (¾ x 36 x 38in)

Brass strip, approx 330 x 90 x 1mm (13 x 3¾ x ¹⁄₂₅ in) (a door kick-plate is suitable)

Thixotropic impact adhesive (allows slight adjustments to be made)

2-part wood filler

Acrylic gold size

Transfer gold leaf

Wax candle

White primer

Straw and mauve undercoat, oil-based

Dark red one-coat gloss (for sundial face and lettering)

White spirit or turpentine substitute

Screws, ½in x No.6

tools and equipment

Sliding bevel

Protractor

Vice

Jigsaw with metal-cutting blade

Half-round, fine-cut file

Emery cloth

Medium-grade glasspaper

25mm (1in) paintbrush

Signwriter's brush or size 4 artist's brush

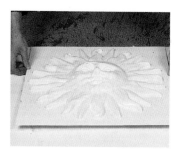

1 Paint the plywood with primer and allow it to dry, then mark the position of the moulding centrally on the board, so that it will sit flush with the top edge. Coat the back of the moulding with impact adhesive (using the spreader provided), and a corresponding area of the board. Leave it to dry for the recommended period in a well-ventilated area – preferably out of doors.

2 Position the top edge of the moulding flush with the top edge of the board and carefully lower the moulding on to the board. Press down firmly all round the flat areas of the moulding. Paint the face and board with grey undercoat.

3 The gnomon must be set at 51 degrees (corresponding to the degree of latitude) below the horizontal. This we achieved by bending out two flanges at the back edge. Mark the centre line along the brass plate, then set a sliding bevel to 51 degrees using a protractor and mark this angle out from the end of the plate on both sides of the centre line. These angled lines are the bend lines for the flanges. Clamp the plate along this line in a vice and bend the flange through 90 degrees by hammering along the line.

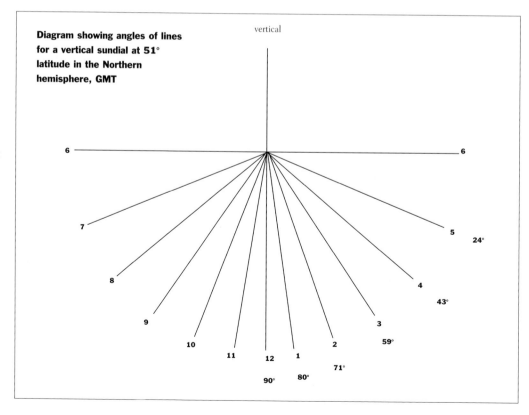

Diagram showing angles of lines for a vertical sundial at 51° latitude in the Northern hemisphere, GMT

vertical

4 After forming the flanges, bend the plate in half lengthways (so that the flanges project outwards). Because of the length, you will need to clamp the plate over the edge of your workbench, with a wide batten on top of it, and bend it over the bench. Mark the outline of the gnomon shape on the brass and cut it out with a jigsaw fitted with a metal-cutting blade. Smooth the edges with a half-round, fine-cut file and finish with emery cloth.

5 Drill a line of holes through the face of the sundial of a diameter equal to the thickness of the bent gnomon, then cut along the holes to form a slot: if using a padsaw, work from the front of the face; with a jigsaw, work from the back – to avoid splintering the plastic. You could fill behind this part of the moulding with expanding foam filler to reinforce it.

6 Drill a hole in the corner of each flange (in our case we used a door kick-plate which was pre-drilled). Pass the gnomon through the backing board from the back (check that it is the correct way up) then screw through these holes into the board to secure it.

7 The angle of the top edge of the gnomon to the board below it should be 39 degrees (or whatever corresponding angle adds up to 90 degrees). You can make small downward adjustments by packing beneath the corners of the flanges with washers cut from polythene bottles. Fill round the gnomon with two-part wood filler and smooth it level with the surrounding surface when dry.

8 Apply a coat of mauve undercoat to the board as a base colour. When this is dry, rub the surface randomly with the edge of a wax candle.

9 Apply the second colour. For this we used straw-coloured full undercoat, but this time we thinned the paint with 1 part white spirits to 4 parts paint. When the paint has dried, rub over the surface lightly with medium grade glasspaper: the base colour should show through the second colour where the wax was applied.

10 Paint the face of the sundial with dark red one-coat gloss and leave it to dry. Brush gold leaf size on to the face and allow it to become tacky. Apply the gold leaf through the paper backing sheet with your fingers, pressing well into curves and crevices.

11 Draw in the lines for the hours at the angles marked on the diagram, using a protractor. First draw the 6 o'clock and the vertical 12 o'clock lines at right-angles to each other, then centre the protractor where these lines cross to mark the other angles. Mark out the lettering and numbers in pencil on the back board. Paint in the details with the one-coat gloss paint, using a signwriter's brush or a size 4 artist's brush.

fire pit

I first saw a fire pit in a dramatic garden in the United States, tucked into a steep hillside overlooking the Mississippi River. Imagine a pit filled with glowing embers, providing a highly convivial focus for eating and chatting around after dark on long summer evenings. The extra warmth encourages you to linger outside and enjoy the night air tinged with a waft of wood smoke.

Fires not only provide a source of fascination for adults, but fuel an endless stream of make-believe games for older children too. We have sited ours near (but not too near) our 'live-in' tree house (see page 140), so that we can cook a simple meal on it, and watch the embers from the balcony.

We have made this fire pit from bricks – reclaimed London stocks, which are a mellow colour and very durable. Alternatively it could be made with stone walls. The floor of the pit is earth. Our soil is very free-draining and so we did not encounter any problems with sitting water when we dug it out. If you are on wet land or have a high water table then drainage might be necessary.

Although our fire pit has been sited in a wilder part of the garden, it could be incorporated near the main outdoor eating area. Then it would be ideally sited to take the chill off the night air for diners on late summer evenings. A different shape, such as a square or rectangle, might fit in more comfortably with a more organized garden format. An alternative is an outdoor gas heater, specially designed for gardens – easier to use, but not quite the same!

MATERIALS

Bricks, 160 approx, special quality
    or engineering
Concrete, 1:6 cement:ballast
Mortar for laying bricks, 1:5
    cement:sharp sand
Mortar for pointing, 1:6
    cement:building sand

tools and equipment

Spray marker paint
Beam compass
Shovel
Brick bolster
Club hammer
Wooden float
Bricklayer's trowel
Pointing trowel

SAFETY

If you have young children, you will
doubtless be aware of safety considera-
tions, both when the fire is lit and unlit
(taking care to cover it when unattended).
And spare a thought for animals that may
stray into the pit, providing them with an
escape ramp if it is left uncovered.

1 Mark out the circle for the pit using a beam compass. Make this from a 900mm (36in) length of batten, and drill a hole 50mm (2in) from one end to take a long bolt; this will give a radius of 850mm (34in). Using a can of spray marker paint (or a narrow paint brush and bright emulsion paint), mark out the circle on the ground.

2 Dig out the hole to a depth of 500mm (20in) for a width of 325mm (13in) within the marked line, and 350mm (14in) deep in the central area.

3 Ram a 75mm (3in) layer of hardcore into the bottom of the circular trench. Make up a stiff concrete mix of 1 part cement to 6 parts ballast and lay a ring, 300mm (12in) wide and 100mm (4in) thick, on top of the hardcore. Level it off with a wooden float and taper the inner edge to support it while it hardens. The surface of the concrete should be 340mm (13½ in) below ground level. When the concrete has hardened, backfill the central area with soil level with the concrete.

4 Drill another hole in the beam compass to give a radius of 600mm (24in), and use it to position two bricks on the concrete 90 degrees apart, butting up to the end of the batten and aligned with it. Dry-lay bricks between these to check the spacing. Lay the first brick on 12mm (½ in) of mortar, mixed from 1 part cement to 5 parts sharp sand, and set it level. Lay each successive brick at an angle to the previous one, using the beam compass to give its position and alignment. The joints taper from about 0 to 25mm (1in).

5 Build up the brickwork with three header courses (bricks laid flat and running in line with the radius) and one soldier course at the top (bricks laid on edge). Stagger the vertical joints by about a quarter of a brick width (25mm/1in). The bottom of the fire pit is compacted soil.

6 Point the joints between bricks with a mortar mix of 1 part cement to 6 parts building sand. Finish the joints flush with the surface of the brickwork. Remove surplus mortar from the face of the brickwork with a stiff-bristled brush when it has started to go off (about one hour, depending on conditions).

serpentine mowing margin

Mowing margins reduce the time spent maintaining the lawn, as they negate the need to edge up the grass with shears. They are particularly appropriate for smaller areas, and provide a well-defined edge that emphasizes the shape of the lawn.

In this woodland area the mowing margin was added not so much for maintenance reasons as to make a design feature to highlight the serpentine grass path. The edge of stone slabs is laid just 10mm (⅜in) or so below the height of the grass to allow the mower blades to run over the paving. As the canopy of the surrounding trees becomes more dense, the lower branches will be trimmed to let light through to the grass and to create an informal archway.

Mowing margins can be formed from many materials to suit the circumstances. Here I have used Indian stone slabs. In rustic areas, railway sleepers cut in half lengthways and sunk marginally below the grass are inconspicuous but hard-wearing and hard-working. Bricks can be used; these are particularly suitable for forming curves and circles. They can be used satisfactorily to form radii as tight as 500mm (20in) by cutting them in half and laying them on end. If you were putting in a margin adjacent to a wide mixed flower border you may want to increase the width of the paved margin to allow the plants to flop on to the paving, so avoiding them being chewed up by the mower. In these circumstances a width of 600mm (24in) may be more suitable.

In many situations it would not be necessary to lay the concrete; the slabs could just be laid with the mortar bed and hardcore. The concrete was added here because of the close proximity to the vigorously growing trees.

MATERIALS

Concrete, 1:5
    cement:ballast
Hardcore
Mortar for laying
    paving, 1:5
    cement:sharp sand
Mortar for pointing,
    1:5 cement:soft
    sand
Indian stone slabs,
    200 x 200 x 50mm
    (8 x 8 x 2in)

tools and equipment

Long measuring tape
String line and pegs
Spray marker paint
Builder's square made
    from 3 pieces of
    batten nailed
    together: 1.2, 1.6
    and 2m (3, 4 and
    5ft) long
Shovel
Metal float
Bricklayer's trowel
Rubber mallet
Pointing trowel
Pointing iron (or
    bucket handle)
Stiff-bristled brush

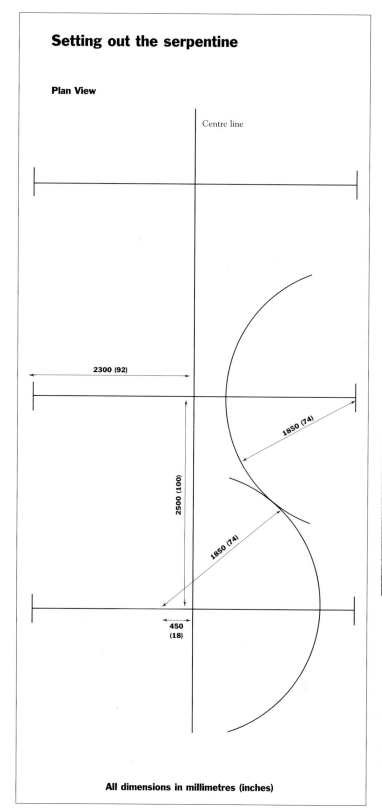

Setting out the serpentine

Plan View

Centre line

2300 (92)

1850 (74)

2500 (100)

1850 (74)

450
(18)

All dimensions in millimetres (inches)

1 Using a string line and two pegs, set out the centre line of the path which will be flanked on both sides by the opposing serpentines. Our line is 17m (56ft) long, but obviously it can be varied to fit your design. Mark along the line with spray marker paint.

5 Dig out the trench, 250mm (10in) wide and 230mm (9in) deep, inside the serpentine lines. The stone slabs we used were 200mm (8in) square, and we had them cut from larger 600 x 600mm (24 x 24in) slabs. They will sit on 75mm (3in) of hardcore and 75mm (3in) of concrete, with a 25mm (1in) mortar bed on top.

2 Set out the parallel lines 2.5m (100in) apart which cross the centre line at right-angles. To set the right-angle, make up a triangular gauge from batten with sides 1.2m, 1.6m and 2m (3, 4 and 5ft) long – a ratio of 3:4:5; the two shortest sides form a right-angle. Mark the lines to extend 2.3m (92in) on both sides of the centre line and keep checking that the distance between the ends of the lines is exactly 2.5m (100in).

3 Draw an outward-facing circular arc, with a radius of 1.85m (74in) and centred 450mm (18in) on the opposite side of the centre line. Use a tape measure and spray marker paint, or a narrow paintbrush and bright emulsion paint. Make the arc rather longer than necessary because, when you set out the next arc, you will see exactly where the two curves marry up sweetly.

4 From the outer end of the next parallel line (2.3m/92in from the centre line), draw an inward-facing arc of the same radius to meet up with the previous arc. Continue in this way to produce the two opposing serpentines. Make sure that the path they form is how you envisaged it. This is the time to make it narrower or wider, or to change the radius of the circles – before you start the harder work!

6 This photo shows the different layers of the construction in the trench: hardcore rammed into the base of the trench, 'blinded' with mixed ballast to fill in the gaps, and topped with concrete. The slabs are laid on a continuous bed of mortar.

7 The concrete base is a mix of 1 part cement to 2 gravel to 3 sharp sand (or 1 cement to 5 ballast). Lay the concrete 75mm thick on the hardcore and trowel off the surface. Leave it to set hard before proceeding.

8 Mix up mortar in the proportions 1 part cement to 5 coarse sharp sand and lay a bed 20-25mm (¾-1in) thick on the concrete. Position the stone slabs and tamp them down to 10mm (⅜ in) below the turf level, using a rubber mallet.

9 The stone slabs must be completely dry for the next stage, or any mortar which gets on to the surface will be difficult to remove. Point between the slabs with a stiff mortar mix of 1 part cement to 5 soft sand, using a pointing trowel. Recess the joints using a pointing iron (a bucket handle makes a good alternative). Promptly brush off any mortar from the surface of the slabs with a stiff-bristled brush.

grass steps

I have included these grass steps, as many gardens have changes in levels and require steps, but 'hard' steps formed from brick, stone or other paving materials would look too intrusive in certain situations. These steps are very wide – about 3.5m (11ft 6in), because of the large scale of the slope and the orangery at the top of it. Obviously the width can be tailored to suit individual sites, though it is important to slope the slabs at the ends of the steps to allow the ends to be mown and negate the need to edge up the grass with shears. A narrow mowing margin has been included at the base of each step for the same reason.

Grass steps look particularly effective when used to climb gently up through flowering meadows or light woodland. An alternative design is to make the risers from plants, such as ivy or box, and put a wide tread of hard material at the top. In this situation the planted riser is usually not a vertical surface but slightly battered, and the tread needs to be at least 400mm (16in) deep (from front to back) to allow it to overhang the softer planted soil but also have the back of the slab resting on a good footing.

Peach-coloured, Indian stone slabs have been used, but reconstituted stone slabs could be used as an alternative. Bricks tend to look more obvious as they are thicker. Timber is a good choice; it is far less expensive but obviously needs replacing at regular intervals. It is also important – but more difficult with timber – to make sure the grass is marginally (approximately 10mm/$\frac{3}{8}$ in) proud of the hard material to allow the mower to run over the top.

MATERIALS

Paving slabs for risers (quantity to suit), 600 x 300 x 50mm (24 x 12 x 2in)

Paving slabs for mowing margin (quantity to suit), 600 x 150 x 50mm (24 x 6 x 2in)

Concrete, 1:5 cement:ballast

tools and equipment

Water-level (optional)

Long straight-edged piece of timber

Long tape measure

String line and pins

White spray marker paint

Timber peg (for marking level)

Shovel

Barrow

Bricklayer's trowel

Rubber mallet

Disc cutter with masonry-cutting blade

Safety gear: goggles; face mask; ear defenders; safety shoes or boots

MARKING OUT AND EXCAVATING

First of all we worked out the total height of the slope in order to calculate how many steps we would need. We used a spirit-level, a long plank and a measuring tape, but you could hire a water-level. First we stretched a string line down the centre of the slope as a line to work to. Then, starting at the top of the slope with one end of the plank resting on the ground, we set it level and measured the height of the other end above the ground. From this point we repeated this process, and so on to the bottom of the slope, to work out the total height and horizontal length; these were 1190 and 5250mm (45½ and 210in) respectively. We checked our measurements by measuring the distance along the slope: this distance squared should equal the sum of the squares of the other two measurements. We decided to make a flight of seven steps, each with a height (rise) of 170mm (6½ in) and a depth of tread (from front to back) of 750mm (30in). A rise of 200mm (8in) would be the maximum, and this is steep. The flight included the final riser from the top of the grass up to the terrace, and the riser here was set into the ground to the same depth as the others but cut to fit under the overhanging edge of the terrace.

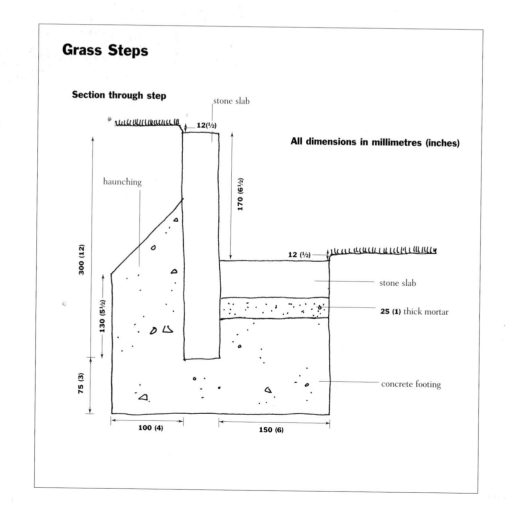

Grass Steps

Section through step

stone slab

All dimensions in millimetres (inches)

haunching

170 (6½)

12 (½)

12 (½)

300 (12)

stone slab

25 **(1)** thick mortar

130 (5½)

concrete footing

75 (3)

100 (4)

150 (6)

1 Mark the ends of the centre line of the steps relative to their final destination and measure out half the width of the flight on both sides of it. Set out the position of the steps, using pegs and a line, and mark each line with spray marker paint.

2 The completed marking out: the repeated pairs of two parallel lines which are close together show the position of the mowing margin, which in this case is the horizontal, 150mm (6in) wide stone slabs. Apart from the bottom one – where no riser was possible because of the shallow gradient – the mowing margins will be backed by the risers to the next level.

3 Divide the turf into strips 300mm (12in) wide using a spade, and cut across the strips every 600mm (24in). Carefully lift off the rectangles of turf for re-use with an even depth of soil (on average 35mm/1½ in, but 25mm/1in is the minimum) and lay them to one side. The edges of what will be the turfed area of the treads slope up to the grass on each side.

Cutting stone slabs

Stone slabs, or flags, are best cut with a disc cutter, which you can hire. By doing it in this way, you will more than offset the cost of the broken slabs resulting from manual methods. It is a noisy, messy job but is not difficult.

✓ Make sure that you understand the operating instructions fully.

✓ Wear the appropriate safety gear: ear defenders; safety goggles; face mask; and safety boots or shoes.

✓ Lay the slab on sound, level ground.

✓ Keep other people – especially children – away from the work area.

4 Dig out 300mm (12in) wide trenches for the risers and mowing margins (see diagram). Each trench should be 375mm (15in) deep below the higher level; and about 200mm (8in) at the front, to coincide with the final level of the top of the mowing margin. The photo shows the completed excavation of the trenches for the first three mowing margins and two risers, and the level areas for two grass treads between them.

5 In most situations, the steps will finish with a mowing margin and riser up to the final level. At the top of the flight in our case there was a raised terrace with an overhanging edge, and so we cut the riser to fit beneath it, making sure that the height of this final step to the surface of the terrace was the same as the other ones.

CONSTRUCTING THE RISERS

Start constructing the steps from the bottom upwards. Set the height of the top of the first riser by knocking a peg into the lower level at the centre of the edge of the first tread, with the top of the peg 170mm (6½ in) above ground level in our case. Then rest a straight-edged length of timber on the peg with a spirit-level on top of it and set the first riser slab to this height. Repeat for the slab on the other side of the step and set up a string line between them. The top of this completed riser will be used as a datum level for the one above, and so on.

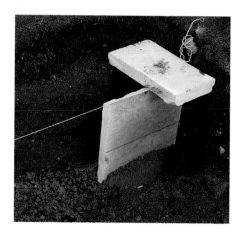  

6 Pour 130mm (5½ in) of concrete into the base of the trench to support the riser. Cut two half slabs for the outer positions, 300 x 300mm (12 x 12in), using a disc cutter (see Cutting stone slabs, page 79); this ensures that the vertical and horizontal joints are staggered. Position them on edge in the concrete and set the height of the top edges by tamping them down with a rubber mallet. Check that the tops are horizontal and stretch a string line between them.

7 Lay full-length slabs between the outer ones, working from both sides towards the centre and aligning the top edges with the string line. At the centre, cut a slab to length to fit the gap.

8 Pour in more concrete behind the riser so that it comes to 120mm (4½ in) below the top edge, and haunch down (angle) the surface at 45 degrees to make sure that enough room is left for topsoil under the turf. Firm down and level the concrete in front of the riser to 245mm (9½ in) below the top edge.

CONSTRUCTING THE TREADS

The ends of the mowing margins slope up to the adjacent grass so that the turf will eventually marry up smoothly. To get this angle, measure 575mm (23in) in from the end of the riser and 170mm (6½in) down from the top and mark the slab; then draw a straight line from this point to the top outer corner of the riser. Mark another line 75mm (3in) below this one and parallel to it; this line marks the level for the top of the concrete, allowing 50mm (2in) for the thickness of the stone slab and 25mm (1in) for the mortar bed.

9 Lay a stiff mix of concrete up to the lower sloping lines and across the trench between them. When the concrete has gone off, lay the sloping slabs on a bed of mortar and tamp them down level with the upper sloping line using a rubber mallet. Firm up the mortar and level it off flush with the edge of the slabs.

10 Stretch a string line between the lower ends of the sloping slabs and hold it in place with offcuts. Lay the horizontal slabs butting up to the sloping ones and tamp them down level with the string line. Check with a spirit-level that they are level from front to back. Lay the remaining slabs, working from both sides towards the centre. At the centre, cut a slab to fit the remaining gap.

11 This photo shows the completed riser and mowing margin. Repeat this sequence to the top of the flight and leave the concrete and mortar to go off overnight. The next day, backfill with the excavated topsoil to make up the levels, firming it down behind the risers. Cultivate and rake the ground in preparation for re-laying the turf.

12 Lay the turf in strips across the treads, working from front to back and staggering the joints between turves in adjacent strips. At the mowing margin, cut the turves to butt tightly up to the slabs, making sure that the top is about 10mm (⅜in) proud of the slabs so that a lawnmower can run over the slabs without damaging the blades. Water it in well, and keep it moist until it has re-established itself.

chequerboard paving

Chequerboard paving can be a stylish and relatively inexpensive way of forming a useful, fairly hard-wearing surface. It can function as a seating area, but because it uses both a hard and a soft surface, the positioning of chairs and tables requires care. It also works as a path, although when it is wet you obviously have to watch where you walk. This is an ideal choice for an undulating site as it disguises the variation in the level – slabs alone would show up every change in angle. The possibilities are not restricted to squares: horizontal bands, triangles and curved patterns can all be woven into a soft blend of green and stone.

Here we have mixed Indian stone paving with grass. The grass sits just proud of the paving (about 10mm/⅜in) so that the mower can run over the top of the slabs without damaging the blades. Other plants that do not need mowing could make a substitute for the grass, such as *Thymus minimus*, *Sagina glabra* or *Chamaemelum nobile* 'Treneague'. The thyme and chamomile have the advantage of a wonderful scent, and all three form neat ground-hugging mats of green, but none of them will take as much wear as grass and, if bald patches appear, new plants will need to be added.

In comparison to a totally paved area, the softer look of the blend of plants and paving can be a big advantage in certain parts of the garden, such as the area shown in the photo: a nuttery underplanted with woodland plants. Other areas where this approach is suitable are wide paths through lawns, around large pools, or for huge terraces.

MATERIALS

Paving slabs, Indian stone, 600 x
   600 x 50mm (24 x 24 x 2in),
   quantity to suit
Hardcore
Mortar, 1:5 cement:sharp sand
Turf

tools and equipment

Garden roller, or punner
Rubber mallet
String line and pins
Barrow
Lawn edging tool

1 The first photo shows the completed
excavation. It runs on both sides of a grass
path and is 150mm (6in) deep (to take
75mm/3in of hardcore, 25mm/1in of mortar
and 50mm/2in thick paving slabs). Compact
the soil using a garden roller or punner (a
300mm/12in square of plywood, screwed to
the end of a length of 75 x 75mm/3 x 3in
timber for a handle, will do the job).

2 Starting at one corner, lay a 600mm (24in)
square of hardcore, 75mm (3in) thick, and
level off the top with a trowel. Check the
dimensions of the square. We used ballast for
the hardcore, which is easy to handle. This,
too, should be well compacted.

6 Trim off any surplus mortar with a trowel,
flush with the edges of the slab, and smooth it
against the base of the slab. Return the
surplus to the barrow. Measure 600mm (24in)
from the edge of the slab and mark a line in
the soil; this gives the starting position for the
next slab. Then trim off the surplus ballast
and use this to form the base for the next
slab. Level the ballast, lay more mortar, and
proceed as before. This photo shows the
strips of mortar.

3 These large slabs were laid on strips of mortar – rather than a continuous bed – so that they could be tamped down into position. The mortar was a mix of **1** part cement to **5** parts sharp sand and it was laid about 50mm (2in) thick.

4 Position the slab over the mortar, aligned with the string line, and lower it horizontally on to the mortar. Don't be tempted to lower one edge first, or the mortar will be compressed unevenly and you will have to lift the slab and start again.

5 Tamp down the slab with a rubber mallet. On a level site, use a spirit-level to check the level. In our case the site sloped in both directions, and the slab had to be set by eye to follow the string line.

7 Prepare the remaining squares for the turf by raking fine soil over them to a finished level about 10mm (³⁄₈ in) below the paving. This will leave the turf slightly above the paving so that it can be mown easily. Lay the turf from rolls and press it firmly down on to the soil with your hands.

8 Where the roll meets the paving slabs, cut through it with a sharp-edged spade or a lawn edging tool. Lay the full widths from each roll first, then lay the infill strips – to maximise the use of the turf and minimise the number of joins.

9 Position the infill strips to butt up tightly against the turf on one edge, and cut them to fit against the adjacent paving.

mosaic paving

Small areas of mosaic paving are fun to do; they can be designed to almost any theme, and, of course, made particularly appropriate to the garden or owner! We used pebbles from two suppliers. The pebbles come graded into various sizes, and we sorted through them to separate the colours (white for the rabbit, darker colours for the surround) and also to select the flatter ones that would butt up to each other fairly tightly. The quarry tiles were standard machine-made ones which we cut up and tumbled with sharp sand to give a softer, warmer feel to their appearance.

It is possible to collect many other types of material for paving mosaics. Angular quarry stone, often sold for hardcore, is a useful filler, although you need to go through a heap of it to select pieces with a flat top. Strips of slate can be used to form lines, similar to the way that the quarry tiles have been used in this project.

The motif could consist of a simple star, geometric shape, initials or compass – all of which can be highly effective. This one is fairly small – only 900 x 900mm (36 x 36in) – and so the base was formed in concrete. The pebbles were set in flush with the surrounding paving setts because water will easily run off this small surface area. However, for a larger area it is good practice to set the pebbles about 5mm (¼ in) higher than the surrounding area so that water runs off it. Larger areas would also need to be laid to a fall to give adequate drainage.

MATERIALS

Indian stone paving setts, 100 x 100 x 100mm (4 x 4 x 4in)

Quarry tiles

Pebbles:

Mixed colour pebbles, 20-30mm (¾-1¼in) and 30-50mm (1¼-2in)

Snowdonia tumbled pebbles, 50-100mm (2-4in)

Hardboard for template, 800 x 800mm (32 x 32in)

Hardcore

Concrete, 1:8 cement: ballast

Building sand, for supporting template

Mortar for laying setts, 1:5 cement:sharp sand

Dry filler material, 1:2:3 cement: sharp sand: 6mm (¼ in) grit

Dry mortar for bedding pebbles, 1:1:1:3 cement:sharp sand: building sand:6mm (¼ in) grit

Dry mortar mix for brushing in, 1:3 white cement:soft sand

Pointing mortar for setts, 1:4 white cement:building sand

tools and equipment

Heavy-duty tile cutter

Jigsaw

Drum and coarse sand (to tumble quarry tiles)

Steel float

Bricklaying trowel

Pointing trowel

Club hammer

Straight-edged length of timber

Soft-bristled brush

Kneeling board, knee pads (optional)

1 The mosaic was destined to sit between two areas of existing paving. We excavated between them to a depth of 260mm (10¼ in), rammed in a hardcore base 75mm (3in) deep, and topped this with 75mm (3in) of concrete. Level off the concrete to 110mm (4¼ in) below ground level (in our case, this was the existing paving).

2 Lay an edging of stone setts to contain the mosaic; the setts are dovetail-shaped and should be laid with the smaller face downwards. Lay a bed of mortar, 75mm (3in) deep, and bed the setts into it. Tamp them down level with the adjacent paving, using a club hammer with scrap wood between it and the setts. Taper the edge of the mortar towards the centre of the area so as to support the setts while it hardens.

6 When you have cut sufficient pieces to edge the template twice round, tumble the tiles in a drum with coarse sand, to take off the sharp edges. We put about 6 shovelfuls of sand in the mixer with the tiles, and tumbled them for about 2 hours. The photo shows the tiles before and after tumbling, and with the sand washed off.

7 Fill inside the border of the panel with building sand and lay the template on top of it. Position it centrally and set it level with the border using a spirit-level and straightedge.

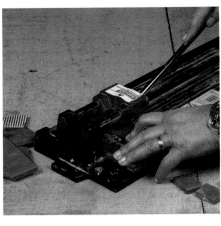

3 The mosaic is formed around a template – in our case a rabbit which we downloaded as clip art from the internet. This we enlarged and copied on to hardboard. Cut out the shape from the hardboard with a jigsaw, making sure that the board is well supported near the cutting position.

4 The template shape will be edged with small pieces of tile. Cut these by first scoring across the surface using a heavy-duty tile cutter, and making sure you go right up to the edges.

5 Then place the scored line under the handle and press down firmly to snap it. You will need some pieces smaller than others to fit in the tight curves.

8 Scoop out the sand round the template in sections and replace it with the dry filler mortar mix of 1:2:3 cement:sharp sand: 6mm (¼ in) grit, to form a wall in which to set the tile edging. The mortar should taper outwards towards the bottom.

9 Set the tile pieces into the mortar on edge, one layer at a time, and tap them down so that the top edge is flush with the template.

10 The completed tile edging: where the shape turns corners, and where the ends meet, you may need to find narrow tiles to fit the gap. Check that there are no protruding edges which could be a tripping hazard.

11 Adjacent to the setts which form the edge of the panel we laid a margin of flat pebbles, set on edge into mortar. This time the mix was 1:1:1:3 cement:sharp sand:building sand: 6mm (¼ in) grit. Tap the stones into the mortar with a hammer until they are level with the setts.

12 Sort the pebbles into shapes for use inside and outside the tile outline of the rabbit. A good-sized kneeling board is helpful, on which they can be sorted. You will also find knee pads a great comfort for jobs such as this.

13 Continue to fill in the area outside the rabbit with smaller, flat pebbles, running parallel to the line of the animal. Keep checking with a straight edge that no pebbles are projecting above the surrounding setts.

14 Fill in the body of the rabbit with oval pebbles, using small ones where the shape dictates. Lay these so that the long axis of each pebble is at about 45 degrees to the direction of the flat stones.

15 Brush a dry mortar mix of 1:3 white cement:soft sand into the gaps between the stones, working parallel to the direction of the lie of the pebbles. Finally, sprinkle water over the whole area using a fine rose on a watering can.

16 Point the joints between the concrete setts with a mortar mix of 1:4 white cement:building sand. The dried pointing will have a similar colour to the setts.

woven archway

This archway is based on a simple metal ogee-shaped arch which can be made up by a local blacksmith to the dimensions shown. It is then woven with hazel and willow to form a small tunnel. The basic idea is to use the metal as a long-term, almost invisible, framework and then to apply the organic material to form a soft-looking but stable and relatively long-lasting structure.

The hazel rods were cut from coppiced hazel stock. If the hazel and willow are cut in the dormant season they should last a good eight to ten years, especially as they are not driven into the ground. They can then simply be replaced, and the framework re-used.

The metalwork was primed and then painted with a gloss paint chosen to match the willow. We fixed the legs into the ground with concrete, but in certain soil conditions it probably could be anchored with rammed earth. The length and width of the archway can obviously be altered to suit the site and the shape of the arch could be Gothic, Roman, Tudor, triangular or three-centred – to name a few options. Alternatively, the same principle could be adapted to form an arbour, and the seat could be made from woven hazel with a chamomile top – an adaptation of the woven tree seat on page 100. The finial could be picked out in gold to add a touch of sparkle to contrast with the otherwise rustic nature of the project.

MATERIALS

Metal archway
  (*see drawing for
  dimensions*), made up
  by a blacksmith
4 tiles or flat stones
Hazel rods, approx 104
  of 3m (10ft) length
Willow wands,
  Salix viminalis, approx
  24 of 3m (10ft) length
Dark olive green gloss
  paint, primer and
  undercoat
Horticultural wire, green
  plastic-coated
Concrete, 1:2:3 cement:
  gravel:sharp sand

tools and equipment

2 planks of wood (to
  support hazel)
2 lengths of bamboo
Rope

1 First tie a length of bamboo across the base of both arches to prevent them from deforming. Work with the archway flat on the ground so that you can compress the woven hazel. Weave the thin end of the hazel in and out of the cross members, feeding in the length as you progress along the frame. Work alternately from the base and the apex, alternating the direction of overlap of the cross members, and build up both sides of the archway simultaneously.

5 The trimmed ends at the apex should form a neat line, overlapping from alternate sides.

2 As you complete each length, trim off the projecting end. The ends should project beyond the apex by 50mm (2in) and form a line 450mm (18in) above the bottom of the legs. (We had to trim off about 30mm/1¼ in). Press the hazel down to compact it.

6 Dig a hole for each leg of the arch, 300mm deep and 250mm square (12 x 10in). Place a tile in the bottom of each hole, and lay a plank of wood between the two holes on each side to support the lower ends of the hazel. Tie the rope between opposite legs to prevent them from splaying outwards and (with help) lower the archway into position. Check that it is upright, then partly fill each hole with a very dry, lean concrete mix of 1 part cement to 2 parts gravel to 3 parts sharp sand, up to 200mm (8in) from ground level. The concrete will keep the arch rigid. Backfill with soil to ground level.

7 The arch frame was disguised by weaving willow wands around them. These had been soaked in water overnight to make them supple. Feed the wands up through the frame from below the third horizontal from the bottom, pushing with one hand and pulling with the other. Wind it round the frame and the first hazel rod, as tightly as the willow will allow, up to the apex.

3 Tie in the lengths which pass outside the cross member at the apex using horticultural wire. Make a single turn of wire round the hazel and the frame and twist the ends together. (When the hazel has been in place for some time, it will keep its shape unrestrained.)

8 Follow the line of the first lengths of willow with subsequent lengths, positioning them side by side. Near the apex, where the willow is thinner, bend it out into a loop to enable you to feed it through the horizontal frame members.

4 Keep checking that the weaving is running parallel to the frame of the arch. Every so often, weave two lengths with the thick end at the base to prevent a build-up of thickness at the apex – where four ends overlap for every two at the base.

9 At the apex, trim the ends to project by about 75mm (3in), with the ends from opposite sides interwoven alternately. Five lengths of willow on each side should cover the metal frame adequately.

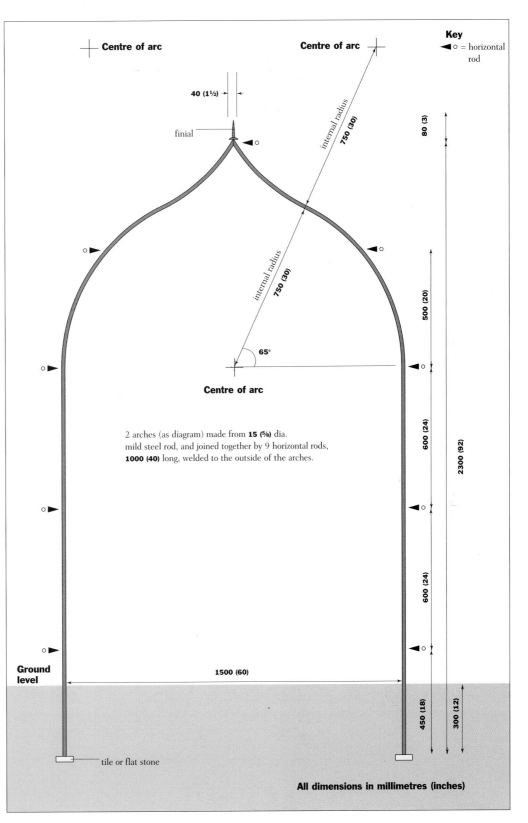

Centre of arc   Centre of arc

40 (1½)

finial

internal radius **750 (30)**

internal radius **750 (30)**

65°

Centre of arc

80 (3)

500 (20)

600 (24)

2300 (92)

600 (24)

2 arches (as diagram) made from **15 (⅝)** dia.
mild steel rod, and joined together by 9 horizontal rods,
1000 (40) long, welded to the outside of the arches.

Ground level

1500 (60)

450 (18)

300 (12)

tile or flat stone

All dimensions in millimetres (inches)

woven oak strip fencing

This unusual and distinctive below-eye-level fence forms a rustic boundary that separates two fairly natural parts of the garden. It is made using 6mm (¼ in) thick sections of oak strips, or veneer, which are about 130mm (5in) wide. The oak strips are woven together and fixed to rustic poles. The photographs show them in their natural colour. This starts off a warm, pale golden colour which slowly weathers down to an attractive pale grey.

The oak should last about ten years or so, but painting it with a clear woodstain would prolong its life further. This fence has been woven with fairly tight gaps – they average about 30mm (1¼ in) both ways. The gaps are by no means uniform due to the varying width of the oak – they range from 20-100mm (¾-4in), which adds to the rustic charm. The bigger the gaps, the easier it is to construct, but this obviously involves a reduction in privacy. If you keep the gaps tight you will find the fence will tend to bow out a little, though again, as it is rustic, this is not really a problem.

It is a fairly easy fence to build, and inexpensive. It could be made 1.8m (6ft) high if privacy was required. The willow woven band, using *Salix viminalis*, along the top is purely decorative – this could be omitted or increased in depth.

MATERIALS

Oak strips, 6mm (¼ in) thick, varying between 100 and 170mm (4 and 7in) wide:
  9 verticals per panel, 1.2m (4ft) long
  5 or 6 horizontals per panel, 1.8m (6ft) long
Posts: softwood stakes with their bark left on, 75mm (3in) dia. x 1.8m (6ft) long
Creosote
Willow wands, *Salix viminalis*, 7 per panel, 1.8m (6ft) long
50mm (2in) galvanized nails
40mm (1½in) panel pins

tools and equipment

Drive-haul (hired) or sledgehammer
Length of 25mm (1in) sq. batten
Jigsaw
Circular saw

1 The fence posts we used were 75mm (3in) diameter softwood stakes; they were 1.8m (6ft) long, to give the fence a finished height of 1.2m (4ft). The bottom 500mm (20in) was soaked in creosote overnight. We hired a drive-haul to drive them 400mm (16in) into the ground, but you could excavate a hole and backfill. Space the posts at 1.75m (5ft 10in) centres. The inside of the drive-haul can be used as the container for treating the base of the posts.

2 First position the bottom three horizontals and nail the ends to the posts with 50mm (2in) galvanized nails. Adjacent lengths should meet centrally over a post. Space the horizontals about 30mm (1¼ in) apart.

USING A DRIVE-HAUL: SAFETY MEASURES

The drive-haul is the purpose-made tool for driving in posts. However, if lifted above the top of the post when in use, it can strike the post at an angle and bounce off, causing severe head injuries.

✓ Wear a safety helmet.

✓ Keep other people, especially children, away from the work area.

✓ Take great care not to lift the bottom of the drive-haul above the post top when driving it in: use only small strokes of the tool.

✓ Adjust your grip on the handle as the post is driven in, to adjust the lift

✓ Ensure that you have a firm footing on stable ground.

6 Now return to the horizontals. Insert the next one at an angle so that it can be woven through the verticals, one by one, as it is lowered into position. When it is woven through, knock down first one end, then the other, and repeat this until it is in position. Ensure that one end is central over the previous post, then nail both ends to the posts, pushing the timber against the post with a length of batten.

7 Put the last horizontal in position. Now, using a jigsaw, cut off the top of alternate verticals flush with the upper edge, to leave the intermediate verticals projecting. This is done because the willow which tops the oak strips is not so flexible and could not be woven through such small distances. Cut off the projecting ends of the horizontals with a circular saw set to a shallow depth.

3 Next insert the verticals, starting next to the previous post. Weave them between the horizontals, overlapping them on alternate sides. The verticals are most easily inserted midway between the posts.

4 Tap the verticals sideways into position using a hammer and a length of 25mm (1in) square batten to protect the edges from damage. The spacing should be the same as for the horizontals – about 30mm (1¼ in).

5 As you near the end of a panel, the verticals become more difficult to weave through. Insert the blade of a spade to guide them through the horizontals, and tap them down with a hammer and timber packing from the top.

8 Weave in the willow (seven strands in all), alternating the direction in which they run so that a thick end is followed by a thin end and so on. Cut the ends centrally over the posts, using secateurs, and pin the ends to the posts with 40mm (1½ in) panel pins. Tap the woven willow down between the verticals so that it lies flat.

9 Cut off the remaining projecting verticals about 25mm (1in) above the woven willow. Cut off the post tops 100mm (4in) above the willow.

woven tree seat

A Lords bench around a conveniently sited tree is a functional and often highly attractive feature. There is not a huge range of them to choose from when buying 'off the peg', and getting one the right size can be problematical. This simple version, made from woven hazel and willow has the big advantage that the design is fairly versatile. The ideal tree is one that is not too huge as it would be more difficult to drive the stakes into the ground, and the soil on top of the roots may be detrimental to a mature tree; a younger tree will easily adapt.

The willow and hazel should be cut in the dormant period – between the end of November and February in the northern hemisphere – as it will last a lot longer if the sap is not flowing when it is cut. They should also be left to dry a little (ideally about six weeks or so) as they tend to shrink after cutting, and it is better to use pre-shrunk material otherwise your gaps will increase in size.

The rustic nature of this seat fits in well in an informal area. It could be in any shape and need not enclose the tree entirely. A back could be made for it by threading longer hazel rods vertically down through the inside circle and then bending them over in a curve and threading them back in vertically further round on the curve. Several rods treated like this could then be interwoven with willow to form an attractive backrest to part of the seat.

The top could be planted with chamomile (*Chamaemelum nobile* 'Treneague') or creeping thymes (*Thymus minimus*), saving the need for cutting the grass. In dry areas the thyme would probably respond better to the conditions than the turf.

MATERIALS

Tanalized fencing stakes with
  pointed ends, 31 of 50mm
  (2in) dia. x 850mm (34in) long
Flexible hazel rods, approx 80 of
  3m (10ft) long or more
Flexible willow wands,
  Salix viminalis, approx 12
  of 3m (10ft) long or more
Water-permeable membrane
  (Mypex, from garden centres):
  1 piece 500mm x 6.5m (20in x
  22ft) for the outside wall
  1 piece 500mm x 4m (20in x
  13ft) for the inside wall
Turf/grass seed to cover approx
  2.2 sq m (24 sq ft)
Topsoil, approx 0.75 cu m
  (27 cu ft)
Water-storing polymer granules

tools and equipment

Spray marker paint
Sledgehammer
Barrow
Pointing trowel

1 Set out the inner circle for the hazel wall. Because the tree is in the centre, you cannot use a line and peg, so measure 500mm (20in) out from the trunk and mark the ground every 200mm (8in) round the circumference using a can of spray marker (or a narrow brush and emulsion paint). Then join up the marks freehand to form a neat circle. Mark a second circle 450mm (18in) outside the inner one.

2 Using a sledgehammer, knock stakes into the ground at 325mm (13in) centres round both circles. The stakes are 50mm (2in) in diameter, with pointed ends, and are 850mm (34in) long to enable 400mm (16in) to be driven into the ground, leaving 450mm (18in) exposed.

6 Cut the turf into squares which will fit between the two rings of weaving. Lay the first square and, at one side, cut out a triangular gusset. A pointing trowel makes a good tool for this.

7 The gusset allows the next square to follow the direction of the seat.

3 Take a hazel rod, its thickest end approximately 25mm (1in) in diameter, and place this thick end outside a stake on the inner ring. Weave it in and out of the ring of stakes; this requires a bit of strength initially but becomes easier as the diameter of the rod diminishes. Carry on building up the height in this way, changing the side of the stakes which are overlapped every two or three layers.

4 Top the hazel with a few lengths of willow wands, woven in the same way. Using a spirit-level, check that the top of the weaving is fairly level. Some adjustment is possible by compacting the weaving where it is high. Trim off the stake tops with a handsaw, flush with the top of the willow. Weave the outer ring in the same way. Try to ensure that both ends of the hazel rods finish between the inner and outer ring of stakes so as to leave a smoothish surface where legs will dangle.

5 To contain the soil between the walls of the seat while allowing water to drain out, place a continuous sheet of water-permeable membrane on the inside surface of both walls, lapping on to the soil at the bottom between them. Fill between the walls with soil containing polymer granules (to absorb water), tamping it down as you progress. Level the surface 12mm (½in) below the top of the weaving and rake it to a fine tilth so that the turf can root easily. Trim off the surplus membrane.

8 Lay the next square hard up against the cut edge and press it firmly on to the soil.

9 Cut the final piece of turf to fit the gap that remains. Finally, water the turf thoroughly with a rose on a watering can. Water it regularly until it has rooted, especially in dry weather.

10 The finished seat. When the grass grows it can be cut with shears or a strimmer.

tree seat

This is one of the simplest projects in the book, and it will transform an ordinary tree into something quite special. It also increases dramatically the area of informal seating that you can provide – always useful when you are invaded by visitors.

The supports for this seat are reconstituted stone balls, which are fairly easy to find from a garden or architectural supplier. They have a flat area – usually to prevent them from rolling, but in our case positioned uppermost for attaching the seat top. For the top itself we used Far Eastern plywood, but marine plywood would be longer-lasting though more expensive. We painted the top with an opaque woodstain in a dark green colour.

There are several ways the look of the bench could be varied – apart from changing the colour both of the balls and of the seat itself. The height could be increased by 50mm (2in) by sitting the balls on small squares of paving stones, perhaps 200 x 200mm (8 x 8in), and bedded on to a small concrete plinth. Instead of using 'stone' balls, roughly rounded timber balls will give a more natural finish. Clipped box balls also look good, and these can be positioned in front of sturdy load-bearing timber legs.

In a small garden, seats tend to command a lot of attention and if you can make or source unusual and eye-catching designs, they can go a long way towards giving your garden a distinctive and original stamp.

MATERIALS

Reconstituted stone balls, 6 of 300mm (12in) dia.

Seat tops: marine plywood, 2 sheets 2440 x 1220 x 25mm (96 x 48 x 1in)

Edging strip: marine plywood, 70 x 4.5mm (1¾ x ³⁄₁₆) x approx 10m (33ft)

Seat bearers: tanalized softwood, 6 of 40 x 200 x 390mm (1½ x 8 x 15½ in)

Screws: 2, 2¼, 3in x No. 8

Masonry fixings for 3in x No. 8 screws

30mm (1¼ in) panel pins

Ballast

Mortar, 1:4 cement:sharp sand

Waterproof woodworking adhesive

Woodstain, opaque dark green

Exterior-grade filler

tools and equipment

Beam compass

Jigsaw

Circular saw (optional)

Shovel

Straight-edged length of timber

Glasspaper

1 The seat is 400mm (16in) wide with an overall diameter of 1900mm (76in) and is made in two halves which are joined together *in situ*. Mark out the curves on to 25mm (1in) plywood using a beam compass: the outer radius is 950mm (38in) and the inner radius 550mm (22in). On the underside of the semicircles, mark the 60- and 120-degree positions. Cut out the pieces with a jigsaw and smooth the edges with a block plane.

2 Screw the seat bearers to the underside of the seat tops, using 2¼ in x No. 8 screws. They run from the outer to the inner curve and are centred on the 60- and 120-degree marks. Two of these bearers overlap the end of one seat top by half their width and will be used to join the two halves together.

7 Roll the ball back into position on the mortar and adjust the position of the flat top so that it is level in all directions. Check that the ball is firmly seated. The flat top of this ball will now be the datum point for setting the height of the other balls.

8 Position the remaining balls in the same way and check the level relative to the datum ball. Excavate until each one is exactly level, then set it on mortar and settle it in by pushing it from side to side until the flat top is level again with the datum ball. You will need to place the spirit-level on a straight-edged length of timber for the further balls.

3 Temporarily lay out the seat tops, centred round the base of the tree, to mark where the stone balls are to be positioned – centrally under the bearers. Remove the seat tops and position the balls with the flat area uppermost. (The 'flat' is already formed on the balls – to prevent them from rolling in normal use.)

4 Lay a spirit-level between each pair of balls in turn and determine which is the lowest one. Use this ball as the starting point. Mark the turf round the ball with the edge of a spade.

5 Roll the ball aside and cut out the circle of turf inside the marked line using a spade. Excavate 100mm (4in) and ram in 75mm (3in) of ballast.

6 Mix up some mortar from 1 part cement to 4 parts sharp sand and shovel it into the circle up to the base of the adjacent grass.

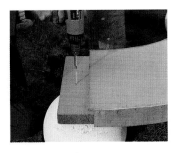

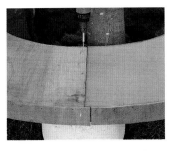

9 Pin and glue the edging strip at 100mm (4in) intervals round the seat, flush with the upper surface. Fix one end then work round the circumference of each curve, pressing the edging into the curve. Plane the top edge so it is flush with the seat and sand smooth.

10 When the mortar has set, position the seat half with the projecting bearers on the balls, and centre all the bearers on the balls. Check that there is an equal overhang inside and outside the seat.

11 Drill through the centre of the end bearers into the balls to mark the position for the screw fixing. Remove the seat and drill and plug the holes to take 3in x No. 8 screws. Replace the seat and screw it to the balls.

12 Position the other seat half with its ends overlapping the projecting bearers. As the balls restrict access from beneath, drill pilot holes for three No. 8 screws per joint through the plywood into the bearers and counterbore them with a larger drill bit so that the screw heads will sit below the surface. Join the two seat halves together with 2in screws. Fill over the screwheads with exterior-grade filler and sand smooth before painting.

awning

Many eating and sitting areas benefit from shade, and an alternative to the large umbrellas is this awning which is very straightforward to make. This one has been made from a large dustsheet, which we have shaped to give it a bit more style. The fabric and size of dustsheets vary tremendously, so it is worth looking at lots and seeing which you prefer. Alternatively, you could buy some canvas and seam it together and then shape it. We added a trim of bias binding (which is available in many other colours), to add some detail and colour, and it could be added to both the underside and the topside, if wished. Bias binding was chosen because it will follow the curve without rucking up.

The mast bands are made from polished gunmetal and they are also available in aluminium from the suppliers we used. This company specializes in awnings and will design and make one for you, if required. The poles, pegs, and tension adjusters (or wood slips), were obtained from a tent manufacturer.

The awning is designed to be put out on sunny days and then taken in when it is wet and windy. If this type of structure is left out in windy conditions, the fabric would exert a lot of force on the hooks in the wall and on the poles, so do not forget to take it in.

The poles with their dark red and gold barber-stripe design, topped with onion-shaped finials, add an exotic touch, but they could be left unpainted or stained in a soft green for a low-key look. The gold paint is easier than gold leaf to apply, but it will dull down when exposed to the elements, so it is a good idea to varnish it.

MATERIALS

Dustsheet, 2.4 x 3.6m (8 x 12ft)

Bias binding (colour to suit),
    13m (43ft)

Strong cotton tape, 1cm (⅜ in)
    wide x 1m (3ft)

Pine poles, 2 of 50mm (2in) dia. x
    2.1m (7ft)

Finials, 2 onion-shaped, with rings

Dowels, 2 of 10mm (⅜in) dia. x
    25mm (1in)

Mast bands, 2 of 50mm (2in) dia.

Wooden tension adjusters, 2 of
    150 x 40mm (6 x 1½in)

Tent pegs, 2 approx 330mm (13in)
    long

Cotton rope, 10mm (⅜ in) dia. x
    8m (27ft)

Concrete, 1:1:3 white cement:
    sharp sand:ballast

Dark red gloss paint, primer and
    undercoat

Masking tape

Ribbon, 4m (13ft) approx

Gold paint

Stainless steel shackles, 4, with
    15mm (⅝in) opening

Plastic waste pipe, 2 of 50mm
    (2in) dia. x 270mm (11in)
    approx

2 substantial hooks for fixing into
    wall

2 heavy-duty 75mm (3in)
    wallplugs

Gap-filling adhesive

tools and equipment

Fibre-tipped pen

String compass

Sewing machine

Mould oil

Old round plastic flower pot,
    approx. 220mm high x 220mm
    dia. (9 x 9in)

Multi-tool with abrasive head,
    planer file or rasp

Bricklaying trowel

Cartridge frame gun

1 The awning is cut from a rectangular dust sheet and is curved at the edges. To mark out the curves, lay out the dust sheet and use a fibre-tipped pen attached to a string compass to mark the cutting lines. Set the peg at the centre of the string compass 4.35m (14ft 3in) from the mid-point of each edge of the sheet. For the short edges we used a radius of 4.52m (14ft 10in); for the long edges a radius of 4.7m (15ft 5in). These radii will vary depending on the size of the sheet: the pen should pass through the corners of the sheet, so set the radius accordingly.

5 Paint the pole and, when it has dried, wind ribbon round it to give a barley-sugar, twisting line. Measure to check that the turns are evenly spaced then secure the ends with masking tape. Mark along both edges of the ribbon with a fibre-tipped marker pen, taking care not to push it out of position on the pole.

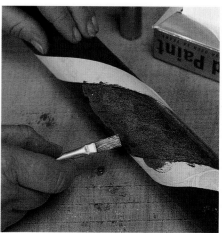

6 Remove the ribbon and wind masking tape round the pole to leave a spiral band where the ribbon was. Paint the exposed band of the pole using a metallic gold paint. When it is touch-dry, peel off the masking tape.

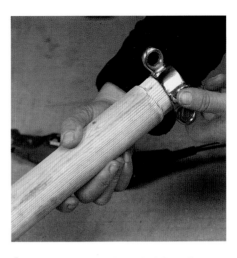

2 The edge of the fabric is double-turned to give a hem 12mm (½ in) wide all round. Bias binding is then sewn to the fabric 12mm (½ in) inside the edge; the weave of the bias binding (at 45 degrees to the edge) enables it to follow the curved edges without puckering. A loop of cotton tape is stitched to each point of the awning and another piece stitched diagonally across the points to reinforce them.

3 To support the corners of the awning we bought pine poles to which we fitted mast bands. These had a slightly smaller inside diameter, so we reduced the diameter of the pole at one end using a multi-tool with an abrasive head fitted. You could also use a rasp or a planer file.

4 Test-fit the ring on the end of the pole: it should be a tight fit when the pole has been painted.

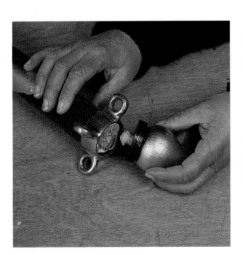

7 Drill the top end of the poles and the underside of the finials to take 10mm (⅜ in) diameter dowel. Insert the dowel in the finial, apply gap-filling adhesive to the top of the pole, and push the finial firmly into position.

8 Pass one end of the cotton rope through an eye in the mast band and attach it by pulling out one strand of the rope and passing the end of the rope under it. Repeat this three more times under every sixth strand.

9 Tape round the bottom end of the rope to keep the strands together, then feed the end through the tensioner from one side and back through the other hole to form a loop for the peg. Tie a figure-of-eight knot in the end of the rope to retain it.

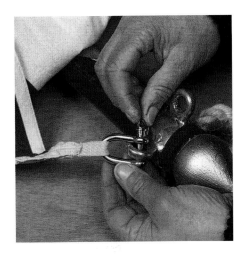

10 Attach the loop of the awning to the opposite eye of the mast band using a screw shackle pin. Thread the shackle through the loop and the eye, insert the pin and screw it home. Tighten it by inserting a spike through the hole in the end of the pin.

11 The back edge of the awning is attached to two screw hooks or eyes fixed in the wall. Drill holes to take 75mm (3in) wallplugs using a masonry drill bit. These need to be positioned slightly further apart than the length of the awning so that it is taut when erected. You may need hammer action if it is hard brick. Drill into the brick itself – not into the mortar joints.

12 Push the wall fixing into the hole and screw in the hook. Pull the hook to check that it is firmly held. The hook we used was coiled, with a black japanned finish.

13 To support the bottom of the pole, we cast concrete feet in a mould made from an old flowerpot with the bottom cut off. Coat the inside of the mould with mould oil (shuttering oil) to aid the release of the concrete.

14 Cut a 270mm (11in) length of 50mm (2in) plastic waste pipe using a hacksaw, to take the base of the pole.

15 Place a piece of board on a level surface and invert the flowerpot on it. Position the pipe centrally in it and trowel concrete around it, using a mix of 1:1:3 white cement to sharp sand to ballast. When you have filled the mould, tap firmly all round the outside with the back of the trowel to release any trapped air and ensure a good surface. Finish the top to a slightly conical shape so as to shed water. Leave the concrete to go off, take off the pot and paint the protruding pipe to match the pole.

trampoline

This is definitely the most popular piece of play and exercise equipment in our garden, and the large 4.25m (14ft) diameter trampoline is big enough for both adults and children to use. Because a large trampoline does not look attractive in a garden we have sunk it almost flush with the ground and mounded the excavated earth around the edge. This conceals it and forms an excellent small amphitheatre from which others can watch while awaiting their turn, and is also thought to be a safer design. To screen the trampoline further, you could plant a screen of shrubs on the outside edge of the bank, but you would have to keep them pruned back so children could not bounce out on to them.

Many trampolines have bright blue plastic edges, but they are also available with the muted olive green surround that we have used, which helps to blend them into the garden. Trampolines also come in various shapes and sizes; this is one of the largest but it still can be tucked unobtrusively into a small town garden. If my experience is anything to go by, it will be used on nearly every dry day throughout the year, and most importantly, it maintains its interest from year to year as the users develop their level of skill. It is extremely vigorous exercise, and a few minutes on this will soon get you puffing.

When we excavated the pit for this, no drainage was necessary. In some areas, however, the depth of the excavation would mean that the hole might partially fill with water, which would necessitate drainage. It is worth digging a trial pit beforehand to see if this will be necessary. The carved logs are an optional extra, adding a touch of fun, combined with extra seating. We used alder logs, but sweet chestnut and lime are also good for chainsaw carving. They should be positioned at least 3m (10ft) from the trampoline or the distance recommended by the manufacturers, whichever is the greater.

MATERIALS

Trampoline, 4.25m (14ft) dia.

Turf/grass seed to cover approx 50 sq m (540 sq ft)

Logs, for dragon seats:

Head section, 1 of 2m x 600mm (6ft 6in x 24in)

Tail section, 1 of 3m x 470mm (10ft x 18in)

tools and equipment

Small digger

Shovel

2 scaffold boards

Chainsaw

Safety clothing

INSTALLING THE TRAMPOLINE

The digger should be used only by a competent operator. Dig the hole to accomodate the trampoline so the top is just proud of the surrounding ground level. Let the sides of the pit fall to their natural angle of repose, covering part of the legs if necessary. We formed the excavated earth into curved banking in the shape of a horseshoe for the body of the dragon, leaving a temporary opening to allow us to escape from beneath the trampoline when it was in position.

1 It takes four people to lift the trampoline, holding it by the legs – this is important, as they are simply a push-fit into the underside of the surrounding ring frame. A further person standing in the hole manouevres it into position as it is lowered down two scaffolding boards. These prevent the soil from being trampled back into the hole and provide a degree of control, as the legs can be slid down them.

2 The height of the trampoline legs enables one to crawl underneath it to make final adjustments to its position (and then to return above ground).

3 Fill in the 'escape hole', and rake the sides of the banking to get a maximum slope of 1:3 in order to facilitate mowing. Flatten the top of the banking and remove any large stones.

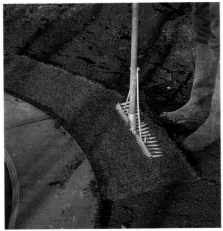

4 The ground next to the trampoline should be either 50mm (2in) above or below the level of the rim, so that mower blades are kept well clear of it. When the level is correct, go over the soil with the back of the rake to leave a smooth surface for the turf.

5 Lay the turf adjacent to the rim first. The large radius of the circle means that the turf can be laid straight from the roll, and will follow the curvature without having to cut gussets. Tamp the turf down (to 25mm/1in below the rim in our case) using the end of the rake. When laying subsequent rings of turf, ensure that the joins between lengths are staggered from those in the adjacent rings.

6 With help, position the head and tail of the dragon (see Making the Dragon) on each side of the 'entrance' to the trampoline, facing away from it. Don't attempt to roll them, or projecting features may break off. Form a mound of earth behind each of them and compact it firmly. This will be levelled and graded into the banking round the trampoline and eventually also covered with turf.

SAFETY: USING A CHAINSAW

✓ A chainsaw should only be operated by a competent adult.

✓ Read the operating instructions carefully and ensure that you understand them fully. If you hire the tool, ensure that the operating procedure is fully explained to you.

✓ Always wear the full safety gear – it should be supplied when you hire the chainsaw. This should consist of: a peaked helmet; visor or goggles; ear defenders; gauntlets; padded leggings; and safety boots.

✓ Tie back long hair, and don't wear loose clothing, which could possibly get caught in the cutting chain.

✓ Ensure that you have a firm footing when working.

✓ Don't allow anyone, especially children, near the area when you are working.

✓ Ensure that the tree trunks are well supported and cannot roll or tilt.

✓ If you are using an electric chainsaw, be sure that it is powered via a RCD-protected outlet: this can be a plug-in safety adapter, a safety socket, or a socket supplied via a RCD-protected power circuit in your consumer unit (fuse box). The chainsaw should be connected to the power lead via a two-part connector which can be easily separated in an emergency.

✓ Obey the drink-drive laws: never operate a power tool after drinking alcohol (however inspired you may feel!).

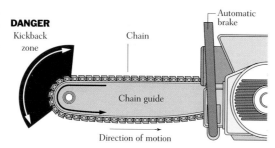

DANGER
Kickback zone

Chain

Automatic brake

Chain guide

Direction of motion

CHAINSAW SAFETY

A Start the chainsaw by placing it on firm, level ground with the chain clear of the ground. Grasp the handle with your left hand and pull the starter cord sharply with your right hand.

B Stand in a well-balanced position on firm ground and hold the chainsaw with both hands. Cut only with the lower part of the chain, avoiding the kickback zone (as shown in the diagram above).

MAKING THE DRAGON

The dragon shape was cut into the logs using a chainsaw, starting at the head end of the larger log. Read the safety notes and captions, and study the diagrams carefully, before starting.

1 Our first cuts produced the shape of the nose, with a horn on top at the front. Next we undercut the bottom jaw (see Making the mouth, right), rolling the trunk through 90 degrees each way to do so. Behind the horn, the top of the nose is flat and smooth to provide one of the sitting positions. There is another flat area behind the ears.

2 The jaw grooves then allow you to cut the teeth, working at right-angles to the axis of the trunk, by giving clearance for the curved end of the chainsaw. First cut down the sides of the teeth: cut the top teeth with the chain vertical (see diagram, cut 5), then cut the bottom teeth with the chain horizontal (see diagram, cut 6). Angle the sides of the teeth at about 75 degrees to the surface.

MAKING THE MOUTH

The mouth is formed in two stages, after forming the shape of the nose (see 1, left). First, cut a V-shaped groove on each side of the nose, working from the front of the nose backwards, and with the end of the chainsaw towards the front. Make one cut from above and one from below, with the plane of the chain guide at 45 degrees to the horizontal (see diagram, cuts 1 and 2). Use the front of the straight part of the chain below the chain guide, and make the cut shallower towards the back of the mouth.

Make a second V-shaped cut into the lower part of the first V (see diagram, cuts 3 and 4), again working from the front of the nose backwards.

The captions to photos 2 and 3 describe how to cut the teeth.

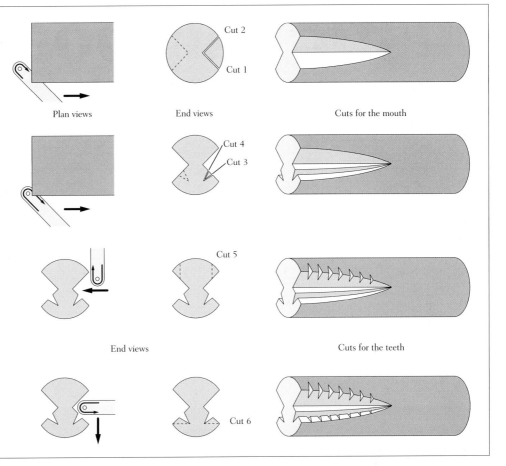

Plan views   End views   Cuts for the mouth

End views   Cuts for the teeth

3 The photo shows the clearance afforded by the two V-cuts which allow the end of the lower part of the chain to be used safely when cutting the teeth. Remove the waste wood from between the teeth with a chisel; the pieces should come out quite easily.

4 The completed head section of the dragon. The scales round the neck were formed with further V-shaped cuts.

5 The dragon's tail has scales along the spine, formed by making V-shaped cuts into the surface. The arrow-shaped end of the tail is formed by making an angled cut on each side towards the tail and then a further cut at right-angles to the surface.

rustic cupboard

This is a useful adapted outdoor cupboard that is designed to stand alone and, if your outdoor space is restricted, could serve as a mini shed. We have kept the height down to 1.8m (6ft) to enable it to fit beside a boundary fence if necessary. The lift-up lid can be propped to give working access.

The work space combined with the sink has been made out of a piece of large cedar, which was obtained from a sawmill. A piece of green oak, as was used for the Oak Table and Benches (see page 126), would be more readily available and less expensive. If you do use green oak, bear in mind that it will leach tannins initially when left outside. These can stain paving slabs and kill vegetation, and so it should be left to stand on an unimportant surface such as gravel which will not suffer, although it can be scrubbed off paving once the leaching has stopped.

We have clad the frame with 6mm (¼in) oak strips which have been left their natural colour. This is a fairly light cladding material that looks good and is quite long lasting. An alternative would be the wavy-edged softwood cladding, as was used on the treehouse doors (page 154); these could be fixed to a thin sheet of external grade ply and then painted with a woodstain.

The sink is a reject butler's sink which has been chipped, but is fine for this sort of situation. A water supply enables you to wash your vegetables and clean them up outside, as well as being ideal for cleaning other items. A shelf could be added above the sink, for storage of pots, pans, watering cans and other useful bits and pieces of gardening paraphernalia.

MATERIALS

All timber is pressure treated, sawn softwood.
Ply is Far Eastern plywood.

Cupboard

Framework, from 25 x 38mm x 20m (1 x 1½in x 66ft)

Front posts, 2 of 50 x 63 x 1400mm (2 x 2½ x 56in)

Front rails, 2 of 40 x 40 x 1200mm (1½ x 1½ x 48in)

Angled side rails, 2 of 50 x 75 x 650mm (2 x 3 x 26in)

Door frames: 8 of 50 x 50 x 1350mm (2 x 2 x 54in)
    8 of 50 x 50 x 300mm (2 x 2 x 12in)

Door braces, 4 of 50 x 50 x 1275mm (2 x 2 x 51in)

Door handles, from oak rail, 2 of 35 x 70 x 700mm
    (1⅜ x 2¾ x 28in)

Back, ply, 1800 x 1200 x 18mm (72 x 48 x ¾in)

Lid, ply, 1200 x 775 x 12mm (48 x 31 x ½in) approx.

Shelves, from ply, 1800 x 1200 x 12mm (72 x 48 x ½in)

Cladding, oak, 6 x 100mm x 60m (¼ x 4in x 200ft)

Roofing felt, 1200 x 800mm (48 x 32in)

Brass butt hinges, 12 of 100mm (4in)

Steel backflap hinge, 1 of 35 x 25mm (1⅜ x 1in)

Steel angle brackets, 3 of 20 x 75 x 75mm (¾ x 3 x 3in)

Clear silicone mastic

Woodscrews: 1in x No. 6; 1in and 2in x No. 8

Panel pins, 19 and 25mm (¾ and 1in)

Galvanized clouts, 12mm (½in)

Workspace

Bearers, 5 of 50 x 75 x 550mm (2 x 3 x 22in)

Posts, 2 of 75 x 75 x 900mm (3 x 3 x 36in) approx

Side supports, 2 of 50 x 100 x 1070mm (2 x 4 x 42in)

End support, 50 x 100 x 200mm (2 x 4 x 8in)

Spacer, 50 x 50 x 200mm (2 x 2 x 8in)

Shelf slats, 6 of 25 x 38 x 1070mm (1 x 1½ x 42in)

Worktop, cedar, 50 x 600 x 1220mm (2 x 24 x 48in)

Splashback, from oak cladding (see above)

Back supports, 2 of 25 x 75 x 250mm (1 x 3 x 10in)

Storage boxes (each):

Sides: 2 of 6 x 100 x 452mm (¼ x 4 x 18in)
    2 of 6 x 100 x 440mm (¼ x 4 x 17½in)

Corner posts, 25 x 25 x 110mm (1 x 1 x 4½in)

Base, ply, 12 x 440 x 440mm (½ x 17½ x 17½in)

Butler's sink, 460 x 620 x 250mm deep (18 x 24 x
    10in) approx.

Brass bibcock, bottom-entry backplate and draincock

Copper pipe, 2m x 15mm dia. (6ft x ½in) approx.

Steel angle brackets, 8 of 20 x 75 x 75mm (¾ x 3 x 3in)

Woodscrews, 1in, 2in and 3in x No. 8

Roundhead nails, 75mm (3in)

Exterior-grade wood filler or timber pegs

Waterproof woodworking adhesive

tools and equipment

Jigsaw

Circular saw

Router (optional) or 12mm (½in) gouge

Power file (optional)

Hole-saw, 32mm (1¼in) dia.

Flat bits, 12 and 15mm (½ and ⅝in) dia.

Smoothing plane

Mallet

Cupboard main frame

The cupboard is constructed around a framework of battens, joined with halving joints to a sturdy front frame on which the doors are hung. Angle braces in the side frames, which are clad only with oak planks, keep the sides square. The plywood back panel keeps the cupboard rigid vertically, and two shelves keep the structure square.

1 Make the top joints of the front frame with halving joints and cut recesses for the side frames. Repeat at the bottom.

2 Screw butt-jointed battens to the plywood back panel. Cut out recesses in the back frame to take the side frames.

3 Join the front to the back by gluing and screwing the side frames into the recesses.

4 Cut and glue angle braces to make the side framework more rigid, ensuring a tight fit.

Cupboard doors

Bifold doors cover the front of the cupboard. These are braced to keep the framework square and are clad with oak planks. Recess the hinges into the door frame members and the front posts. After hanging the doors, plane the meeting edges of the two inner doors until the doors sit flat against the front rails.

5 Exploded corner joint of door frame, showing halving joints. Mark to the actual width and thickness of the frame members, mark half the thickness, and cut with a fine-toothed saw.

6 Glue and screw the joints together using two staggered 2in screws per joint for rigidity. Drill a pilot hole and insert one screw per joint, then check for square and insert the second screw.

7 Hinge the bifold doors together with brass butt hinges: use two hinges for the bifold doors and three hinges to join them to the fixed framework.

8 To prevent the doors from distorting, cut a diagonal brace for each door, to run from the bottom corner on its hinge side to the opposite top corner. Measure while the doors are in the closed position. Glue and screw them in position, flush with the outer face of the doors.

Cupboard lid

Access to the top of the cupboard is via a hinged lid. In this case the battens are butt jointed and serve to add rigidity to the plywood cover. The lid, when resting on the closed doors, sets the slope of the angled side rails of the main frame.

9 The lid framework has butt joints at the corners, and is kept square by two angle braces. An angled batten below the front edge locates in front of the closed doors and prevents them from swinging open (see diagram).

10 Screw the plywood lid to the framework. Cover it with roofing felt fixed with galvanised clouts at 300mm (12in) round the perimeter. Temporarily fit the lid (see step 14).

11 Cut the angled side rails to fit the slope of the lid. Fix them by screwing through the back into the upper end, and using 90-degree brackets bent up to 125 degrees at the front.

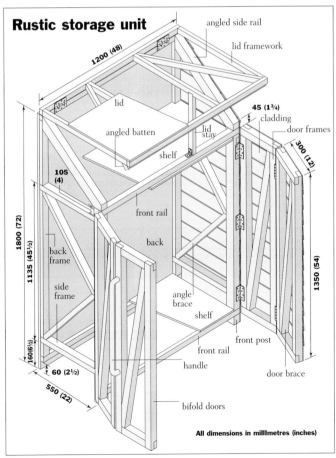

Rustic storage unit

angled side rail

lid framework

1200 (48)

45 (1¾)

cladding

door frames

lid

angled batten

lid stay

300 (12)

shelf

105 (4)

front rail

back

1800 (72)

1350 (54)

1135 (45½)

back frame

side frame

angle brace

shelf

front post

160 (6½)

front rail

door brace

60 (2½)

handle

550 (22)

bifold doors

All dimensions in millimetres (inches)

Cladding the cupboard

If you are also constructing the sink and worktop, refer to stage 1 in the section **Workspace** (right) before cladding the frame of the cupboard, as the bearers for this unit must be fixed directly to the cupboard framework before completing the cladding.

13 The oak handles were cut out of a 35 x 75mm (1⅜ x 3in) oak rail using a jigsaw and were then sanded down to give a rustic but smoother finish. From inside the door upright, drill clearance holes for No.8 screws, then counterbore them with a 12mm (½in) diameter bit to a depth of 25mm (1in). Screw on the handles using 2in x No.8 screws.

15 Make a stay for the lid by hinging a batten to the front top frame member with a backflap hinge so that, when vertical, the batten butts up to the underside of one lid batten. Cut a shallow recess in the lid batten to take the top of the stay and, on the hinge side, screw a small metal strip cut from a steel bracket to prevent the stay from being knocked sideways.

12 Clad the frame, working from the bottom upwards. Scribe and cut each board before fitting it, and overlap the boards by about 25% of their width. Clad the doors across the complete width, then cut through at the centre (where the doors meet) and at their hinge positions with a circular saw; set the cutting depth to the thickness of the cladding.

14 Hinge the lid to the framework using two brass butt hinges. Attach one leaf of each hinge to the lid first, then prop the lid in the open position while fixing the other leaves to the framework.

16 Clad the lid with oak planks, working from the edges inwards to ensure symmetry. The planks were laid in two overlapping layers, some of them being cut with a wavy edge. A bed of silicone mastic makes the covering more waterproof, and the boards are fixed to the lid with 25mm (1in) panel pins.

Workspace: Framework and sink

The workspace is supported on bearers attached to posts at one end (to form a ladder frame) and to the cupboard at the other. The sink depth determines the height of the top cupboard bearer.

1 Make up the ladder frame to the dimensions in the diagram using halving joints. Recess the top of each post so the sink fits snugly between them and cut the top of the posts to be flush with the rim of the sink.

3 Cut the shelf battens to length and space them evenly between the posts. Nail them on edge to the bottom bearers with 75mm (3in) roundhead nails.

5 Position the sink side supports on the bearers and screw the spacer between them on the cupboard bearer. Secure the other arm of the angle brackets at this end. Cut out the top edge of the sink end support to fit round the waste and fit it between the side supports on the ladder frame bearer.

2 Use the ladder frame to set the height of the bearers on the cupboard. The top edge of the top bearer should be flush with the post tops. Fix the bearers to the cupboard framework with 3in x No.8 screws.

4 Screw angle brackets to the underside of each sink side support, set back from the ends by the thickness of the bearers.

6 Wedge two blocks between the side supports and the posts. Check that the ladder frame is vertical and secure the brackets.

7 Position the sink on the side supports with the end of the sink squarely on the end support.

Rustic cupboard workspace

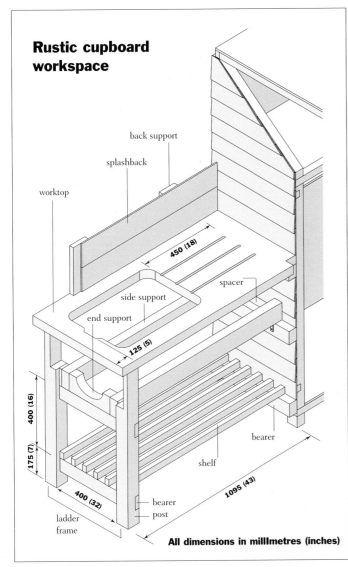

- back support
- splashback
- worktop
- side support
- end support
- spacer
- 450 (18)
- 125 (5)
- 400 (16)
- 175 (7)
- 400 (32)
- bearer
- shelf
- 1095 (43)
- bearer
- post
- ladder frame

All dimensions in milllmetres (inches)

Storage boxes

1 The lift-out boxes have three finger holes in opposite sides. Drill these with a 32mm (1¼in) diameter hole-saw in an electric drill. This gives a smooth edge to the holes, but sand smooth any surface roughness.

2 Construct each box on a plywood base, by pinning and gluing the sides to the edge of the base and to 25mm (1in) square corner posts. The ends of two opposite sides overlap the other two.

Workspace: Worktop

8 Measure the inside of the sink and mark the shape centrally in the width of the worktop. Drill a starting hole for the jigsaw blade inside the line, then cut out the hole in the worktop. Support the central area while cutting.

10 Sand down all edges of the worktop using a power file or glasspaper.

9 To make the channels in the draining board we used a router. If you do not have access to one, use a gouge or else omit the channels. To use a router, set up a gentle ramp from three lengths of batten, 10mm (⅜in) thick. Clamp a further batten to the worktop to guide the edge of the router baseplate and ensure that the channels are straight. Move the router down the ramp so the channel increases in depth from 3mm at the top of the board to 12mm at the end (⅛ to ½in). Secure the worktop to the bearer and posts with a bracket at each corner. Make a cutout at the front corner to clear the cupboard doors when they are open.

11 Make a splashback for the worktop to support a brass tap (known as a 'bibcock'). Cut two recesses in the back edge of the worktop to take the 25 x 75mm (1 x 3in) back supports and screw them in position. Screw or peg oak planks to the supports, with the edges butting up to each other. Fill over the screwheads with exterior-grade wood filler.

12 Screw the backplate of the bibcock through the top plank to one of the supports and fit the bibcock. The copper pipe can be run to it through a hole drilled in the worktop. Fit a drain cock to empty the pipe in winter.

oak table and benches

The outdoor eating area is frequently the most-used part of the garden. Because of this, I like over-sized furniture that can accommodate a sudden influx of unexpected guests, or every member of the family with spread-out newspapers and cups of coffee.

This solid oak table is a simple design that will blend with a traditional farmhouse or a modern town house. The rough-sawn green oak can be ordered pre-cut and, although a hardwood, it is surprisingly inexpensive – especially when compared to manufactured furniture.

This design is extremely chunky, which I think gives it character. However, if preferred, lighter looking sections of timber, such as 150 x 150mm (6 x 6in) for the table legs and a 50mm (2in) thickness for the top, could be used. Because the benches are so heavy, it is advisable to fix them together to prevent them from tipping over and causing damage if they are to stand on anything other than a flat surface; they could be bolted to paving through angle brackets. Due to both their weight and size, the table and benches should be positioned where required and not be moved. If you do need to move them, this can be done by taking the planks off the table one by one and then moving the base, but this is not something to be done on a regular basis.

Green oak does move and split as it dries out, so not only will the colour weather from a golden yellow to a pale, silvery grey but cracks will appear, and this all adds to its appeal. The surface of the table and benches could be sanded down with a floor sander and fed with linseed oil if a smoother look is wanted.

WARNING
Green oak is extremely heavy – weighing 1.25 tonnes per cubic metre (925lbs per cubic foot), so get help when lifting the larger components.
Fresh-cut oak leaches tannins when exposed to rain. To avoid staining paving brown and killing grass and other vegetation, stand the furniture on a gravel area for a few weeks until no more tannin leaches out when it rains or alternatively clean the paving when the leaching has stopped. Beware of leaving tools and other metal items on the oak until it has weathered, as the tannin will stain them very quickly. All metal fixings should be of stainless steel; they are available from boat chandlers.

MATERIALS

All timber is green oak.

Table:

Top, 3 of 75 x 400mm x
    3000mm (3 x 12 x 120in)

Legs, 4 of 200 x 200 x 675mm
    (8 x 8 x 27in)

Cross braces, 2 of 75 x 100 x
    600mm (3 x 4 x 24in)

Cross rails, 2 of 30 x 75 x
    800mm (1¼ x 3 x 32in)

Longitudinal brace, 1 of 75 x
    100 x 2190mm (3 x 4 x
    87½ in)

Longitudinal rails, 2 of 50 x 75
    x 2400mm (2 x 3 x 96in)

Locating battens: 2 of 30 x 75 x
    400mm (1¼ x 3 x 16in);
    4 of 30 x 75 x 200mm (1¼
    x 3 x 8in)

Benches:

Top, 2 of 75 x 300 x 3000mm
    (3 x 12 x 120in)

Legs, 4 of 200 x 200 x 375mm
    (8 x 8 x 15in)

Bench stabilizers, 2 of 30 x 75
    x 1850mm approx (1¼ x 3
    x 74in)

Oak dowel, 13mm (½ in) dia.,
    total length 3.5m (11ft)

Waterproof woodworking adhesive

Stainless steel woodscrews, 2½ in
    x No. 8

Stainless steel coach screws, 8 x
    70mm (5/16 x 3in)

tools and equipment

Wood drill bit, 13mm (½ in) dia.

Sash cramp

Adjustable spanner or socket set

MAKING THE TABLE LEG ASSEMBLIES

1 Mortise-and-tenon joints are used to construct the leg assembly. Mark out the mortises in the table legs to the dimensions shown in the drawing. Drill a hole at each corner of the mortise, **60mm (2³/₈ in) deep** and **13mm (½ in) diameter**, using a wood bit; you can stick adhesive tape to the drill bit as a depth gauge.

2 Chisel out the mortise to the depth of the holes: first work round the edges of the mortise, with the bevelled edge of the chisel inwards, to cut the outline.

3 Then chisel out the bulk of the waste from side to side, with the bevelled edge facing downwards.

4 Finally, pare away any surplus at the sides of the mortise, again with the bevelled edge facing inwards.

Oak table and benches

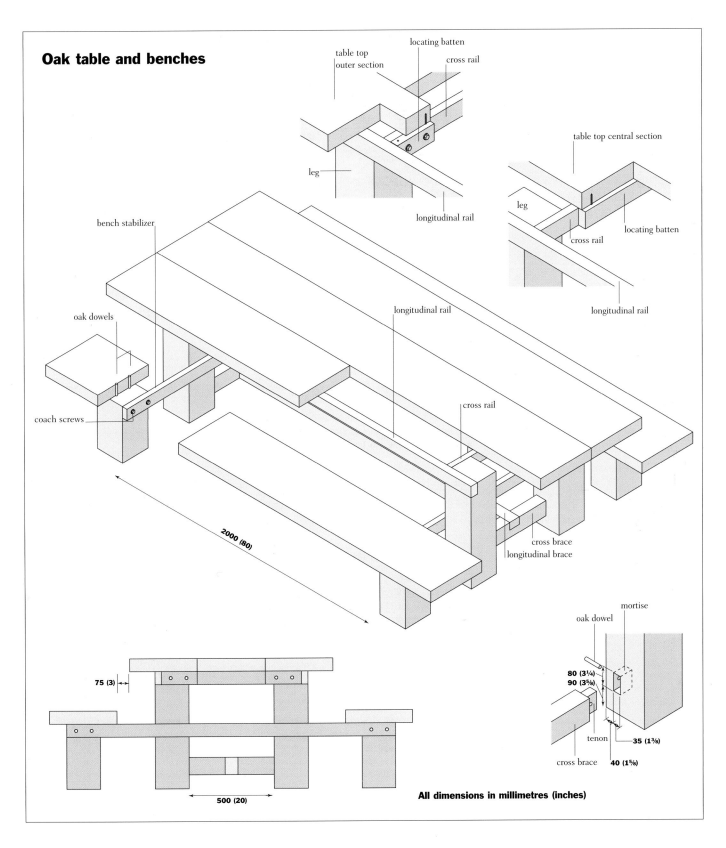

table top outer section

locating batten

cross rail

leg

longitudinal rail

table top central section

leg

cross rail

locating batten

longitudinal rail

bench stabilizer

oak dowels

coach screws

longitudinal rail

cross rail

2000 (80)

cross brace

longitudinal brace

75 (3)

500 (20)

mortise

oak dowel

80 (3¼)

90 (3⅝)

tenon

35 (1⅜)

cross brace

40 (1⅝)

All dimensions in millimetres (inches)

5 Mark out the shouldered tenon (with a rim all round it) on each end of the cross brace. The tenon itself is 80mm high by 35mm wide (3⅛ x 1⅝in), centred on the end of the cross brace. Cut in to the depth line from two opposite sides.

6 Then cut down from the end to the base line. Cut the other two shoulders on the tenon in the same way.

7 Check the tenon for fit in the mortise, and adjust by paring away small slivers until it is a tight fit.

9 At the top of each table leg, cut the two recesses at right-angles to each other – one for the cross rail, and one for the longitudinal rail which connects the two leg assemblies. Mark out the recesses so that the rails (on edge) will stand proud of the leg tops by 3mm (⅛in) and give a level surface for the table-top planks to rest on. Form the recesses by first cutting down to the baseline from the top of the leg, then cutting along the baseline.

10 Assemble the mortise-and-tenon joints and check that the cross brace is square to the legs. Cut the cross rail to fit between the outer recesses for the longitudinal rails. It is fixed to the legs in two planes: to the top and face of the recesses. Drill three clearance holes into the edge of the cross rail at each end, counterbore them with an 8mm (⅜in) drill bit to a depth of 45mm (1¾in), and screw the rail to the top of the recesses. Then drill holes 65mm (2½in) deep for two dowels at each end and dowel the cross rail to the face of the recesses. The photo shows the completed assembly.

11 Cramp up the bottom of each leg assembly with a sash cramp, check that the brace is still square to the legs, and drill a hole 100mm (4in) deep for a dowel, through the inside face of the leg into the mortise-and-tenon joint.

ASSEMBLING THE TABLE AND BENCHES

8 The completed mortise-and-tenon joint. When the leg assemblies are in position under the table top, the cross braces (which are not central on the legs) will be towards the inside. Cut a halving joint in the centre of each cross brace, to take the longitudinal brace.

13 Set out the two leg assemblies 2000mm (80in) apart and with the cross braces inwards. They should be parallel, and the tops should form a rectangle: check by measuring the diagonals, which should be equal. Cut the longitudinal rails to length. Position them in the recesses in the leg tops and drill 100mm (4in) deep dowel holes at 50mm and 130mm (2in and 5in) from each end. Hammer in dowels as before and cut them off flush.

14 Cut the longitudinal brace to length: it should run to the outer faces of the two cross braces. Cut a halving joint at each end and assemble the joints, checking again that the whole structure is square. Dowel the halving joints together with one dowel per joint and saw off the dowels flush with the surface.

12 Hammer a dowel fully into each joint and cut it off flush. It is worth waiting a few seconds to allow any air to escape, then hitting the dowel again, before cutting it off.

15 Screw the locating battens to the underside of each table top through counterbored holes (as in step 10). These battens sit inside the cross rails: on the central top section the battens run the full width; on the two outer top sections they run from the inner edge up to the longitudinal rail. Position the top sections on the leg assemblies and screw the four outer battens to the cross rails using two coach screws per batten.

16 Make the benches by doweling the tops to the legs with two 150mm (6in) long oak dowels per leg. Set the benches each side of the assembled table, at the required distance from the table top, and cut two stabilizers to run from outside face to outside face of opposite bench legs. Position them tight up to the underside of the bench tops and screw them to both legs using two coach screws per leg. Sand the stabilizers smooth and round off the edges. On hard paving, the benches could be bolted down through angle brackets screwed to the inside of the legs.

trellis hedge house

Garden buildings or structures are a great opportunity to have a bit of fun. It is not necessary to slavishly stick to the style of your house because often they do not relate directly to the main building. There is a lot of scope to provide something a little quirky – especially if, as here, it is tucked away at the end of a pleached hornbeam tunnel. The idea is to plant the trellis walls inside with hedging. We opted for hornbeam here, so that the hedging can grow up to form the walls and even be trained along horizontal wires at the top to form a ceiling. When the trellis starts to fall to bits the hedge will have matured and you have the option of either removing or replacing the former.

The style of the trellis house looks quite grand, but the size is very modest – about 2.4m x 1.8m (8ft x 6ft) – so it can be contained in a modest sized garden. The mirror is designed to create an illusion, so that you are tricked into believing that the garden extends beyond. We painted the trellis with a dark blue opaque woodstain, and picked out the finials in a paler blue, with the balls on top in aluminium leaf.

If you had a fence at the back of your garden you could just build the front face of the structure and put in the mirror between the archway, which would then create the illusion of an archway leading on to another space beyond. Because the structure then would only be in one plane it would probably be a good idea to extend the main posts by 600mm (24in) and concrete them into the ground.

We have put a 215mm (9in) wide brick soldier course around the base to position the posts on and provide a firm level base. Alternatively this could be compacted gravel or a narrow band of paving stones.

MATERIALS

All timber is pressure treated, prepared (PAR) softwood. Sizes are actual sizes.

Posts, 28 of 44 x 44 x 2225mm (1¾ x 1¾ x 89in)

Top rails, 2 of 35 x 44 x 2400mm (1⅜ x 1¾ x 96in)

Bottom rails, 4 of 35 x 44 x 800mm (1⅜ x 1¾ x 32in)

Side rails, 8 of 35 x 44 x 1400mm (1⅜ x 1¾ x 56in)

Temporary side battens, 4 of 35 x 44 x 2000mm (1⅜ x 1¾ x 80in)

Spacer battens, 134 of 35 x 44 x 100mm (1⅜ x 1¾ x 4in), including 2 for spacing the trellis slats

Trellis edge battens, from ramin beading 15 x 15mm x 30m (⅝ x ⅝in x 100ft)

Mirror edge battens, from ramin beading 15 x 15mm x 5m (⅝ x ⅝in x 16ft)

Trellis slats, from timber 8 x 34mm x 106m (⁵⁄₁₆ x 1⅜in x 355ft)

Arches, from timber 18 x 225mm x 3.6m (¾ x 9in x 12ft)

Back panel, Far Eastern plywood, 1960 x 900 x 12mm (78½ x 36 x ½in) approx

Post caps:

6 of 20 x 220 x 220mm (¾ x 8¾ x 8¾in)

2 of 20 x 110 x 220mm (¾ x 4⅜ x 8¾in)

Finials, from timber 20 x 225mm x 17m (¾ x 9in x 57ft)

Ball finials, 6 of 65mm (2½in) dia.

Dowel, 300mm x 5mm (12 x ¼in) dia.

Mirror, cast mirrored acrylic, approx 800 x 1925mm (32 x 77in) – measure size before cutting

Steel angle brackets, 16 of 20 x 75 x 75mm (¾ x 3 x 3in)

Bricks or paving for base, as required

Woodscrews: 1¼in x No. 6;

1¼in, 1½in and 2½in x No. 8

Panel pins, 20mm and 30mm (¾in and 1¼in)

Woodworking and building adhesives

Jotuns Demidekk opaque woodstain or similar

Hedging plants, 16 of *Carpinus betulus* (hornbeam)

tools and equipment

Jigsaw

Circular saw (optional)

Mitre saw

Smoothing plane or power planer

Mallet

Cartridge frame gun

Main framework

The front and back walls are constructed using halving joints to connect the posts and rails. Use the dimensions on the diagram to mark out the position of the joints, and the width and thickness of the timbers to gauge the width and depth of the joints. The joints should be cut to half the thickness of the timber in each component. Cut 28 posts to a length of 2225mm (89in). Mark out the positions of the rails and the spacer battens on one post and use it as a template to mark the remaining posts. One of the rails can be used in the same way as a template for the other similar rails.

1 Cut halving joints in the posts and rails to make up the front and back walls. The top pair of rails runs the whole width of the structure; the bottom rails finish at the two centre posts.

2 Assemble the posts and rails to make up the walls. Tap the joints together with a mallet and screw through the posts into the rails with one 1½in x No.8 screw per joint.

3 The pairs of posts in the front wall, and the outer pairs in the back wall, form one half of the towers. Form the other half by clamping and screwing through two posts into the ends of 100mm (4in) spacer battens at the heights shown in the diagram, using two screws per end on the diagonal.

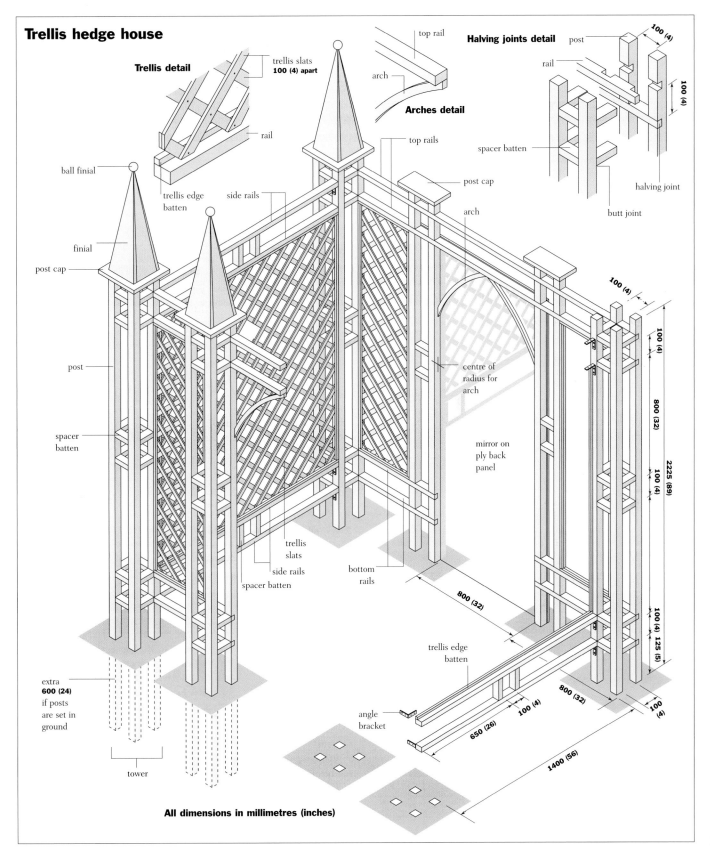

Trellis hedge house

Trellis detail

trellis slats **100 (4) apart**

rail

top rail

arch

Arches detail

Halving joints detail

post

100 (4)

rail

100 (4)

spacer batten

halving joint

butt joint

ball finial

trellis edge batten

side rails

top rails

post cap

arch

finial

post cap

centre of radius for arch

post

mirror on ply back panel

spacer batten

trellis slats

side rails

spacer batten

bottom rails

extra **600 (24)** if posts are set in ground

trellis edge batten

angle bracket

tower

100 (4)

100 (4)

800 (32)

100 (4)

2225 (89)

100 (4)

125 (5)

800 (32)

800 (32)

100 (4)

650 (26)

100 (4)

1400 (56)

All dimensions in millimetres (inches)

4 Fit two further spacer battens at each of these heights to link the two halves of the towers together. Screw at an angle into the posts to secure them, to avoid coinciding with the other screws.

5 Clamp the two halves of the towers together and screw the free ends of the spacer battens to the posts in the front and back walls. Fit two more battens in the centre of the fourth side of each tower and between the each pair of centre posts on the back wall.

Trellis panels

Photos 6 to 8 show how the trellis panels that form the side walls are made. The same principle applies to the panels in the front and back walls of the house. Lay the wall framework flat to construct the trellis. To support the slats, pin 15 x 15mm ($\frac{5}{8}$ x $\frac{5}{8}$in) battens inside the main framework, flush with one face. Position each trellis slat at 45 degrees to the framework and mark its length and the cutting angles. Fit all the slats sloping in one direction first, then add the second layer at right-angles to them. A mitre saw will make this part of the job very much easier.

7 Cut each trellis slat to length, mitring the ends to 45 degrees, and pin them to the edge battens with 20mm (¾in) panel pins. Use two spacer battens, 100mm (4in) long, to ensure that the slats are evenly spaced and parallel.

6 The side wall framework is constructed with butt joints between the rails and the vertical spacer battens. The pair of rails at the top and bottom is held in position by two temporary side battens nailed to the ends. Fix the trellis edge battens with 30mm (1¼in) panel pins, but don't knock the pins fully home in the temporary battens.

8 Where the slats overlap, pin through the centre with the shorter panel pins and bend over the end of the pin to clench the slats together.

9 Fit 90-degree angle brackets flush with both ends of the side rails, ready to connect the side walls to the corner towers. Orientate the brackets for fixing to the top and bottom rails on the front wall, and to the posts on the back wall (see the diagram on page 135).

Gothic arches

10 Mark the centre of the opening on the underside of the lower top rail in the front wall. Lay the wall flat (with the towers uppermost) over an 18 x 225 x 900mm (¾ x 9 x 36in) board. Take a length of picture wire and tie a nail at one end and a pencil at a distance of 825mm (33in) from it. Position the nail on the inside edge of one centre post, about 720mm (28¾in) below the lower top rail, so that the pencil just touches the centre mark on the rail. Draw a curve on the board from the mid-point of the rail to the opposite post. Repeat the process with the wire 25mm (1in) shorter. Then mark where the post intersects the board, and the centre line at the apex. Repeat for the other side of the arch.

11 Using a jigsaw, cut out first the inner curve, then the outer curve, and finally the flat side where the arch meets the post. Take care that the board is well supported near the cutting area. Glue and pin the arch to the posts and rail, flush with the inner face. The two sections of the arch should meet at the centre mark on the rail. Make a similar arch for the mirrored back panel (see 18, page 138).

Erecting the walls

Cut a sheet of plywood to fit across the two centre posts of the back wall and the lower top rail. Screw the ply to the back edges of the framework with 1¼in x No.8 screws. Fit the trellis to the front and back walls before erecting them; this will also improve the rigidity of the walls.

12 Stand the assembled front and back walls on a prepared level brick base, 220mm (9in) wide, set on soil. Prop the walls temporarily with battens nailed to the top rails.

14 Before the trellis side walls can be fitted, you must remove the temporary side battens. Prise out the nails in one batten with a claw hammer and tap the batten away from the trellis edge batten. The trellis is by no means rigid in this state, so care is needed when handling it. Remove the other temporary side batten in the same way.

13 Cut the post caps to size. The caps can be slightly larger than the base of the finials – in which case the top edges should be chamfered to shed water – or flush all round. Position each cap centrally on top of the tower and screw through it into the ends of the posts. Make rectangular caps for the inner pairs of posts on the back wall.

15 The photo shows the side wall trellis panel (on its side), ready for fixing to the towers.

16 Stand one side wall trellis panel in position – either flush with the outside edge of the towers (as shown here) or to leave the towers projecting (as in the diagram on page 135). Support the panel on timber offcuts beneath the bottom side rail so that the rails in adjacent walls align, and check that the side wall is vertical. Attach the brackets to the rails or posts with one screw in the centre hole.

17 Adjust the position of the brackets as necessary, to correct any misalignment of the rails, then insert the remaining screws. Pin through the edge battens of the side trellis into the posts at about 250mm (10in) intervals. Fit the other side wall trellis panel in the same way. You can now remove all the temporary props.

18 Cut a sheet of mirrored cast acrylic to fit snugly between the centre posts on the back wall and up to the lower top rail, with about 2mm (³⁄₃₂in) clearance all round, as described for the False Stone Window, page 51. Cut 15mm (⁵⁄₈in) square batten to run from the lower top rail to the ground on both sides, and another length to fit between these. Apply a bead of gap-filling adhesive across the width of the mirror every 300mm (12in). Position the mirror on the ply and pin the battens to the posts and rail to secure it.

Making the finials

To form the pyramids we marked the 20 x 225mm (¾ x 9in) timber into triangles along its length. For each pyramid, we used four triangles, two with a height of 680mm (26¾in) and a base width of 220mm (8⅝in), and two with the same height but a base width of 180mm (7⅛in). Using a jigsaw we cut out the triangles. In order to fit the triangles snugly together we planed the top two thirds of the inside of each triangle away in a graduated fashion, from the full thickness at the base to a thickness of about 5mm (¼in) at the top. This was done a little bit by trial and error, testing the fit at intervals as we went. Finally we slotted the dowel of the finial into the top and then glued and pinned them together using panel pins.

19 Mark each face of the finial on to the board, to form a triangle with a sharply pointed apex. Cut along the sides with a jigsaw.

20 Two opposite faces of the pyramid must be reduced in thickness towards the apex so that it will have a pointed top. We used a power planer for this, set to a shallow cut, and worked towards the apex in passes, gradually decreasing in length until the apex had virtually no thickness to it.

21 Assemble the pyramid with 25mm (1in) panel pins – seven or eight per edge.

22 Stand the pyramid upright and drill down into the apex with a 5mm (¼in) diameter drill bit, to form a fixing for the ball finial. Drill a corresponding hole in a 65mm (2½in) diameter ball finial and glue in a length of dowel so that at least 15mm (⅝in) still protrudes.

23 Inject some woodworking adhesive into the hole in the pyramid, apply further adhesive to the ball finial around the dowel, and fit it in position. The ball is quite insecure until the adhesive has set, so tape it in position with masking tape.

24 Fit the pyramid finials to the post caps using building adhesive from a cartridge. Apply a bead of adhesive round the top of the post cap, bearing in mind that there is no base panel to the pyramid.

25 Position the pyramid on the adhesive and press it down firmly. Fill round the edges (where necessary) with more adhesive, and smooth it off with a wet finger.

Planting the hedge
26 We used hornbeam for the hedge inside the trellis. Set the plants 450mm (18in) apart and plant them by digging a trench 150mm wide and 225mm deep (6 x 9in), backfilling as you position them.

teenagers'
treehouse

This is the largest project in the book and it is not for the faint hearted! However, the construction techniques are fairly basic and the level of skills required is not too complex. The house is large enough to accommodate some lightweight bunks or airbeds, for additional sleeping space in the summer months. The small balcony provides a wonderful space for relaxing up in the leafy canopy.

You should check the house over at regular intervals – ideally not less than twice a year – to make sure that all the fixings and timber are sound and secure.

The basic house is made from Far Eastern plywood. Marine plywood would be a longer-lasting but more expensive alternative. The plywood has been clad in a range of different materials to illustrate various possibilities. These range from the extremely light pre-formed plastic mouldings made in the form of log rounds which can be painted to resemble the real thing, to thin hazel coppice, wavy boards, thin sections of log rounds laid flat and half-log rounds tacked horizontally. The roof has been clad with willow thatch using *Salix viminalis*, but sedge thatch, half-logs (as on the walls) or bundles of long birch twigs would also work well.

This house does not have any of its load taken by the tree, but is built around the trunk. The tree does need to be fairly substantial, though, so as not to be visually dwarfed by the structure. Avoid trees which look in poor health, or young ones that are growing extremely fast. Willows, robinias and horse chestnuts tend to lose limbs rather unpredictably so they are not a good bet. Large mature fruit trees can be ideal. It may well be necessary to prune the tree to accommodate the house, and if you damage any roots when you put in the posts, do remember to water the tree well in subsequent dry periods.

MATERIALS

see under individual sections

All timber is pressure treated sawn softwood unless otherwise specified.

tools and equipment

Access tower or scaffolding
Extension ladder, 6m (20ft) extended
Step-ladder
Chainsaw
Tree saw
Shovel
Jigsaw
Circular saw
Socket spanner set
Smoothing plane
Chisels
Mallet
Flat wood bit, 25mm (1in)
Cartridge frame gun

SECTION 1:
Constructing the platform

MATERIALS FOR PLATFORM

Posts, 6 of 100 x 150 x 2700mm (4 x 6 x 108in)
Cross beams, 2 of 75 x 200 x 3540mm (3 x 8 x 140in)
End beams, 2 of 50 x 200 x 3280mm (2 x 8 x 130in)
Sub-joists, 3 of 50 x 200 x 3540mm (2 x 8 x 140in)
Joists, 11 of 50 x 75x 3280mm (2 x 3 x 130in), at max. 350mm (14in) centres
Trimmers, as required, each 50 x 75 x approx 700mm (2 x 3 x approx 14in)
Decking boards, with grooved surface, 25 lengths 35 x 150 x 3000mm (1⅜ x 6 x 120in)
Balustrade posts, 8 of 100 x 100 x 1285mm (4 x 4 x 51⅝in)
Facing strips, 3 of 35 x 100 x 1285mm (1⅜ x 4 x 51⅝in)
Balustrade rails, 50 x 50mm (2 x 2in) x 17m (56ft) total length
Ladder rails, 2 of 47 x 100 x 3100mm (1⅞ x 4 x 124in)
Ladder rungs, 8 of 38 x 75 x 800mm (1½ x 3 x 32in)

Angle braces:
8 shaped from 50 x 200 x 1150mm (2 x 8 x 46in)
4 shaped from 50 x 200 x 850mm (2 x 8 x 34in)
Dummy angle braces (optional), 4 shaped from 50 x 200 x 1150mm (2 x 8 x 46in)

Coach screws:
24 of 70mm x 10mm dia. (2¾in x ⅜in dia.)
12 of 160mm x 10mm dia. (6in x ⅜in dia.)
Coach bolts, 8 of 200mm x M10 (8in x ⅜in dia.)
Timber connectors, double-sided, 8 of 50mm (2in) dia.
Joist hangers, as required around tree, to take 50 x 75mm (2 x 3in) joists
Countersunk woodscrews, ½ in, 2in, 2½in, 3in and 4in x No. 8
Rustproof nails, 32mm, 50mm, 75mm and 125mm (1¼in, 2in, 3in and 5in)
Concrete for post footings, 1:6 cement:ballast (if required by ground conditions)
Coarse aggregate

Platform assembly

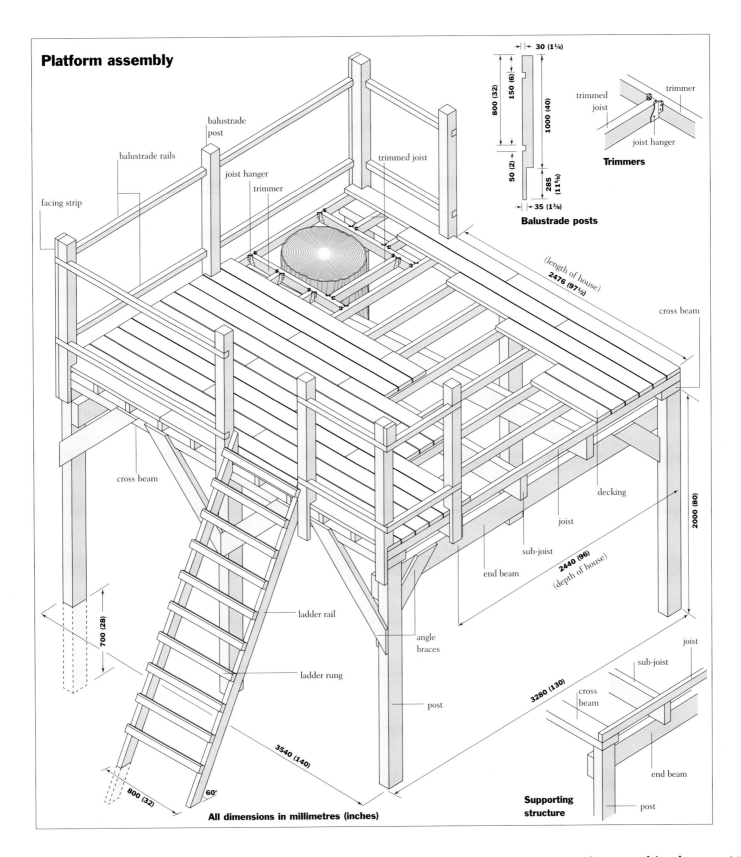

balustrade post

balustrade rails

joist hanger

trimmer

trimmed joist

facing strip

30 (1¼)

800 (32)

150 (6)

1000 (40)

50 (2)

285 (11⅝)

35 (1⅜)

Balustrade posts

trimmed joist

trimmer

trimmed joist

joist hanger

Trimmers

(length of house)
2476 (97½)

cross beam

cross beam

decking

joist

sub-joist

end beam

2440 (96)
(depth of house)

2000 (80)

ladder rail

angle braces

700 (28)

ladder rung

post

joist

sub-joist

cross beam

3280 (130)

end beam

3540 (140)

800 (32)

60°

post

Supporting structure

All dimensions in millimetres (inches)

Posts and beams

We set out the tree house by fixing the position of the four corner posts, positioned with the narrower face on the most frequently viewed elevation, to make them as unobtrusive as possible. They were arranged so that the outer corners would coincide with the corners of the platform. Locating the exact positions and getting the four posts parallel, upright and in a rectangle was one of the most awkward jobs.

We dug the posts 700mm (28in) into the ground, backfilling the holes with well rammed coarse aggregate. In our soil conditions they were quite rigid but in less favourable ground conditions it would be necessary to put in concrete footings, 500 x 500 x 600mm deep (20 x 20 x 24in deep). We fitted two middle posts to provide extra support for the two cross beams. These were centred between the corner posts on the long sides.

The cross beams fixed to the post tops provide end support for the floor joists. In order to allow the use of small-section joists across the 3m (10ft) span, we provided intermediate support by attaching two end beams to the inside face of each pair of end posts, with the top edge 125mm (5in) below the top of the posts. We placed timber connectors between the beams and the posts, but instead you could cut a shoulder about 12mm (½ in) deep at each end of the beam to sit up against the face of the post. On top of the end beams we fitted three sub-joists; the top of these must be level with the top of the cross beams. The sub-joists should be fairly evenly spaced and not more than 1m (39in) apart, but in our case the position of the tree made the gaps a little uneven.

1 Set out the posts 700mm (28in) into the ground within the corners of a rectangle 3540mm (140in) side to side by 3280mm (130in) front to back. Check the vertical in both directions as you backfill the holes. To ensure that the posts sit parallel to each other, you can nail temporary battens across the outside faces.

2 Lay two cross beams flat across post tops on the long side of the rectangle, flush with the outer face of the posts. Drill pilot holes through the beams into the post ends to take the 160mm (6in) coach screws. Counterbore the holes using a 25mm (1in) flat bit so the heads will sit just below the surface.

3 Check the positions of the cross beams, then screw them in place with the coach screws, using a socket spanner.

4 Drill clearance holes in the end beams for the 200mm (8in) coach bolts and counterbore them so that the nuts will sit flush. Rest each beam on a temporary batten nailed to the end posts, 325mm (13in) below the post tops, and drill through the holes into the posts. Remove the beam to complete the clearance holes through the posts.

5 Insert the coach bolts from outside the posts. To reinforce the joints, place a timber connector on each bolt, between the beam and the post. Screw on the nuts tightly over flat washers and cut off the protruding bolt ends flush with the timber.

Joists and decking

The floor joists span across the two cross beams and three sub-joists at a maximum of 350mm (14in) centres. As the tree trunk was in the way of the joists, we inserted a trimmer in the back corner, at right angles to the end two floor joists, and positioned this 50mm (2in) from the tree trunk. This allows for a little growth from the ash tree, which is mature and so is growing relatively slowly. For a more vigorous tree a larger gap would be necessary to avoid the tree growing into the timberwork in the near future. The trimmer was fixed to the two adjacent joists using a joist hanger at each end. A further one in the middle enabled another short trimmed joist to be fitted, in order to give adequate support to the ends of the decking boards adjacent to the tree.

The decking has a ridged surface to make it less slippery in wet conditions. The boards were laid across the joists, leaving small gaps between them for drainage. As they are too short to span the entire length, we cut them to join on the centre of a joist and, to prevent them all joining on the same joist, we staggered the join from side to side. If you need to fit short boards to complete a run, these should span at least three joists.

1 Set out the floor joists at a maximum of 350mm (14in) centres, at right-angles to the cross beams. Skew-nail them to the cross beams and sub-joists with 100mm (4in) roundhead nails. Support the joists while nailing to prevent them from moving.

2 Around the tree trunk you will need to fit trimmers to support the cut ends of the joists. Support these by nailing joist hangers to the adjacent joists with galvanized nails.

3 Cut the trimmer to a tight fit and insert it in the hangers, then nail through the sides of the hangers. Fit the remaining joists, with their cut ends supported in hangers attached to the trimmers. When all the joists are in place, hammer the protruding top ends of the joist hangers flat on to the top of the joists.

4 Fix the decking boards at right-angles to the joists with two 2in countersunk screws into each joist. Space the boards 10mm (⅜in) apart to allow drainage, using an offcut as a gauge, and drill pilot holes for the screws. You may need to cut one or both of the outer boards lengthways to complete the decking.

5 Shape the decking to fit round the tree by scribing round the trunk against a wood block. Butt the decking board up against the tree while scribing, then cut to the scribed line with a jigsaw. Pull the board away from the tree to leave a 25mm (1in) gap for movement and growth. Check the gap regularly.

6 The ends of the shaped decking boards must be adequately supported: no more than 50mm (2in) at the centre of the boards should overhang. An additional short trimmer and trimmed joist may be necessary to achieve this.

Balustrade posts and rails

The balustrade posts are recessed at the bottom end to form a shoulder that sits on the decking. The 35mm (1⅜in) thick projection below the decking is screwed to the joist ends, and to the cross beams where present. In order to strengthen the three corner posts and allow the balustrade rails to sit flush with the posts in both directions, a 35mm (1⅜in) thick facing strip was cut for each of these posts. This runs the whole length of the post and is fixed to the face of the post that is flush with the edge of the platform.

The balustrade rails are set flush with the outer face of the balustrade posts by cutting halving joints 30mm (1¼in) deep in the posts and 20mm (¾in) deep in the rails. On the corner posts, the ends of the two adjoining rails are mitred at 45 degrees.

For safety, all sharp edges of the balustrade posts were chamfered with a block plane and smoothed with medium-grade glasspaper when the balustrade was complete.

1 After cutting the recesses in the balustrade posts (see detail diagram, page 143), hold each post vertically in position and drill pilot holes for 4in screws into the joist ends, and the into the cross beam where appropriate.

2 Insert one of the bottom screws, check that the post is vertical, then insert the top screw. Finally secure with the other three screws.

3 Cut the balustrade rails to length, remembering to leave a gap at the entrance position. Cut halving joints 20mm (¾in) deep where the rails meet the posts. At the corner posts, mitre the ends to 45 degrees. Screw the rails in place with two 2in screws at each joint.

Bracing the platform

After erecting the balustrade, we fitted angled braces to give more rigidity to the platform structure – four on the front and back, and two on each side.

At the front and back, the braces are fixed to the posts and cross beams (see below).

At the sides of the platform the braces are recessed to half their thickness on opposite faces – so as to fit inside the posts and outside the end beams and provide the best support. For appearance, you could add dummy braces on the surface to match those on the front of the platform.

1 To improve the rigidity of the platform, cut 45-degree angle braces to fit between the beams and the posts. Recess the ends by 15mm (⅝in) where they meet the platform and the posts, to form a shoulder, and fix them in position with two 70mm (2¾in) coach screws per station.

Ladder

The ladder rails are set at an angle of 60 degrees to the ground, resting against the decking, and with the 100mm (4in) face against the central balustrade posts. The base of the ladder is set into the ground 300mm (12in) and secured by backfilling with well-rammed coarse aggregate. The top ends are notched over the decking by cutting a bird's-mouth joint and fixed to the balustrade posts, then cut flush with the rear face of the post. The total width of the ladder is 800mm (32in).

1 After setting the base of each ladder side rail into the ground, mark the position of the top of the decking on the inner edge of the rail. Mark and cut a bird's-mouth joint below this line so the rails sit over the decking. Screw each rail to its balustrade post with three 4in screws.

2 Cut the rungs to the outside width of the rails and round off the edges with a plane. Working from the bottom upwards, screw them to the rails 250mm (10in) apart, with two staggered screws at each end. The top rung should be above the decking, 25mm (1in) below the top of the side rails.

SECTION 2: Constructing the house

MATERIALS FOR HOUSE

Far Eastern hardwood plywood, 2440 x 1220 x 18mm (96 x 48 x ¾in):

Walls, 8 sheets, cut to 2000 x 1220 mm (80 x 48in)

Roof, 3 sheets, 1 cut to 2 pieces 2440 x 605mm (96 x 24in)

Gable ends, 1 sheet, cut to 4 triangular panels

Batten, 25 x 38mm (1 x 1½in) x approx 50m (165ft) total length, cut to various lengths

Stiffeners to strengthen doorway:

2 of 50 x 50 x 1975mm (2 x 2 x 79in)

1 of 50 x 50 x 1000mm (2 x 2 x 40in)

Cross braces:

1 of 50 x 75 x 2440 (2 x 3 x 96in)

1 of 50 x 75 x 2404 (2 x 3 x 94½in)

Ridge board, 1 of 50 x 100 x 2476mm (2 x 4 x 97½in)

Roof crown post, 1 of 50 x 75mm x approx 1100mm (2 x 3in x approx 43¼in)

Roof struts, 2 of 50 x 75mm x approx 885mm (2 x 3in x approx 35in)

Balustrade spindles, approx 38 x 38 x 950mm (1½ x 1½ x 38in), cut from 38 x 200mm (1½ x 8in) boards, total length approx 15m (50ft)

Rustic softwood planks with bark edging, 25mm (1in) thick x variable width 200-250mm (8-10in):

Barge boards, 4 of 1925mm (76in) long

Fascia boards, total length approx 14m (46ft)

Cladding:

Front wall: hardwood rustic log rounds, eg beech, approx 260 of 15-25mm (⅝-1in) thick, cut from logs of 50-150mm (2-6in) dia.

Side and back walls: bark-clad log strips, approx 75 of 25mm (1in) max. thickness x 100mm (4in) wide x 2m (79in) long

Gable ends: coppiced hazel twigs, approx 100 of 10-15mm (⅜-⅝in) dia. x 3m (10ft) long

Door: softwood planks cut to wavy edge, 11 x 150mm (7⁄16 x 6in), total length approx 11m (36ft)

Trellis lattice over windows: wavy effect cut from prepared all around (PAR) batten, 10 x 38mm (⅜ x 1½in), total length 14m (46ft)

Roofing felt, 4 lengths 2.6 x 1m (9ft x 3ft 3in) wide

Thatch, willow cuttings (*Salix viminalis* or similar), approx 520 of max. 15mm (⅝in) dia. x approx 2.4m (8ft) long

Garden wire, green plastic-coated, 2 of 60m (200ft) reels, 1mm (0.04in) dia.

Galvanized wire, 10m x 0.75mm (0.03in) dia.

Manilla rope to cover wire, 12mm (½in) dia., 45m (150ft) total length

Clear acrylic sheeting, 2mm (5⁄64in) thick:

Gothic window, cut from 500 x 800mm (20 x 32in)

Windows in doors, 2, each cut from 300 x 850mm (12 x 34in)

Roof truss clips, 2 for 50 x 100mm (2 x 4in) ridge board

Butt hinges, brass, 4 of 100mm (4in) and ¾in screws to fit

Straight barrel bolt, brass, 1 of 75mm (3in)

Door latch with ring handle, 1 of black iron

Screws and nails: some sizes as for platform

Annular ringshank nails, 75mm (3in)

Galvanized felt nails, 20mm (¾in)

Galvanized nails, 50mm (2in)

Panel pins, 20, 25 and 40mm (¾, 1 and 1½in)

Galvanized staples, 20mm (¾in)

Oval nails, 12mm (½in) longer than thickness of barked strip cladding

Woodstains:

Jotun's Oxan woodstain, colour Antikk (for 'ageing' wood)

Drab grey/brown to paint plywood which is to be clad

Forming the house wall panels

Each wall of the house is formed from two sheets of plywood, each sheet being cut down with a circular saw to form a panel 1220 x 2000mm (48 x 80in). The two panels will be fixed together with battens, forming a wall 2000 x 2440mm (80 x 96in), but the final fixing together is better done on the platform. To facilitate this, we screwed the battens to the panels before erecting the walls, using 1½in screws at 300mm (12in) centres. In the following descriptions, 'left' and 'right' refer to the panels as seen from inside the house. The side walls overlap the ends of the front and back walls, and allowance needs to made for this when positioning the battens.

Back wall

Bottom batten Full length of wall, fixed with 25mm (1in) face to left panel, flush with left and bottom edges.

Centre batten Butts up to bottom batten and stops 19mm (¾in) below top of panel, fixed with 38mm (1½in) face to left panel, overlapping right edge by 19mm (¾in).

Corner battens (two) Butt up to bottom batten and stop 19mm (¾in) below top of panels, fixed with 38mm (1½in) face to left and right panels, flush with left and right edges respectively.

Front wall

Form the door by first laying the two panels together on the floor to form the 2000 x 2440mm (80 x 96in) wall. Mark out the sides of the doorway, 1000mm (40in) wide, centred on the wall. It has a segmental arch at the top, the radius of which is 650mm (26in). To obtain this, we formed a beam compass from a piece of batten, drilled a hole to take a pencil through the centre of one end and then hammered through a nail 650mm (26in) from the centre of the hole. With the point of the nail on the centre line of the door, 1150mm (46in) up from the base of the panels, and a pencil in the hole, draw the arch on both sides of the centre line to meet the sides of the doorway. Before cutting out the doors, mark them and the adjacent panels to show which door fits in which panel – in case there is any variation in shape. Cut out the two doors with a jigsaw and put them to one side.

Bottom batten Full length of wall, fixed with 25mm (1in) face to left panel, flush with left and bottom edges. (Portion across doorway cut out after installation.)

Centre batten Runs from 50mm (2in) above doorway to 19mm (¾in) below top of panel, fixed with 38mm (1½in) face to left panel, overlapping right edge by 19mm (¾in).

Corner battens (two) Butt up to bottom batten and stop 19mm (¾in) below top of panels, fixed with 38mm (1½in) face to left and right panels, flush with left and right edges respectively.

Plain side wall

Bottom batten Length of wall less 112mm (4½in), fixed with 25mm (1in) face to left panel, set in 56mm (2¼in) from left edge and flush with bottom edge.

Top batten Length of wall less 86mm (3½in), fixed with 38mm (1½in) face to left panel, set in 43mm (1¾in) from left edge and overlapping top edge by 19mm (¾in).

Centre batten Fits between bottom and top battens, fixed with 38mm (1½in) face to left panel, overlapping right edge by 19mm (¾in).

Window wall

Form the window by first laying the two panels together on the floor to make the 2000 x 2440mm (80 x 96in) wall. Draw a horizontal line to mark the window base, 900mm (36in) from the bottom of the wall and 500mm (20in) long, centred on the wall. Then draw two perpendicular lines, up 370mm (14¾in) from each end of the base, to give the window sides. The Gothic arch was drawn using the beam compass again, with the nail moved to give a radius of 500mm (20in). Position the nail point at the top of one side of the window and draw an arc from the top of the opposite side to the apex of the arch. Move the nail to the top of the other side and repeat the process. Cut out the window with a jigsaw.

Bottom batten Length of wall less 112mm (4½in), fixed with 25mm (1in) face to left panel, set in 56mm (2¼in) from left edge and flush with bottom edge.

Top batten Length of wall less 86mm (3½in), fixed with 38mm (1½in) face to left panel, set in 43mm (1¾in) from left edge and overlapping top edge by 19mm (¾in).

Centre batten (in two parts) One fits between bottom batten and the base of the window, and the other fits between the apex of the window and the top batten; fixed with 38mm (1½in) face to left panel, overlapping right edge by 19mm (¾in).

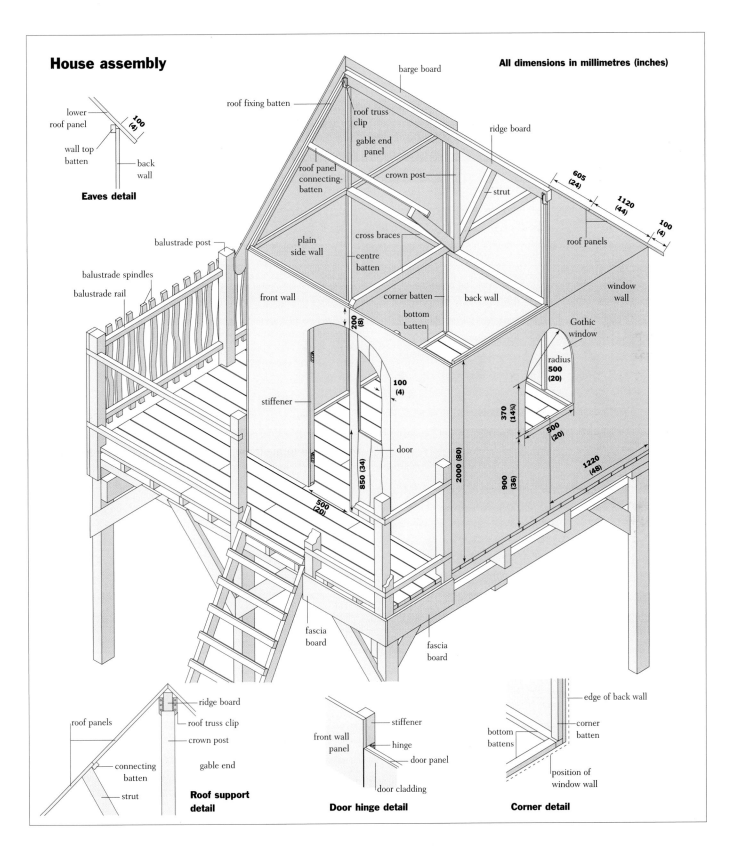

House assembly

Eaves detail
- lower roof panel
- 100 (4)
- wall top batten
- back wall

- barge board
- roof fixing batten
- roof truss clip
- gable end panel
- ridge board
- crown post
- strut
- 605 (24)
- 1120 (44)
- 100 (4)
- roof panels
- roof panel connecting batten
- cross braces
- plain side wall
- centre batten
- window wall
- balustrade post
- balustrade spindles
- balustrade rail
- front wall
- corner batten
- back wall
- Gothic window
- bottom batten
- 200 (8)
- radius 500 (20)
- 370 (14¾)
- 100 (4)
- stiffener
- 900 (36)
- 2000 (80)
- 500 (20)
- door
- 850 (34)
- 1220 (48)
- 500 (20)
- fascia board
- fascia board

All dimensions in millimetres (inches)

Roof support detail
- roof panels
- ridge board
- roof truss clip
- crown post
- connecting batten
- gable end
- strut

Door hinge detail
- stiffener
- front wall panel
- hinge
- door panel
- door cladding

Corner detail
- edge of back wall
- corner batten
- bottom battens
- position of window wall

Erecting the walls

Our house sits on the back right-hand corner of the decking (as seen from in front), as this fitted our particular situation, but this must obviously be tailored to individual trees and circumstances. Ensure that you have stable access when erecting the walls, and work in calm conditions, as the panels become difficult to control in a wind.

We started by assembling the left-hand side wall, and took the first panel (with the protruding battens) up on to the platform. Position it with the outside face 2476mm (97½in) – the length of the house – from the right-hand side of the decking and exactly parallel to it, and with the back corner flush with the back of the decking. With one person holding the panel vertical (using a spirit level), screw through the bottom batten into the decking and joist beneath with 4in screws at approximately 300mm (12in) centres. Take up the second panel and marry it up, checking that the top is flush, then fix it to the protruding battens with 1½in screws at similar centres.

Next fit the two back panels in the same way, flush with the back of the decking and butting up to the side wall. Join the two walls at the corner by screwing into the left-hand vertical batten on the back wall. Working round the perimeter, complete the other walls.

To make the structure more rigid, we put in two 50 x 75mm (2 x 3in) cross braces at right angles to each other, centrally at the top of the walls. The upper one goes from front to back and is fitted with the 75mm (3in) dimension vertical; it is angled at the top corners to accommodate the roof panels later on. The lower brace is fixed, with the 50mm (2in) dimension vertical, between the top battens on the side walls. This may mean bending up the ends slightly – but it is preferable to notching out the underside of the upper brace, which would weaken the support for the roof provided by the crown post and struts (see page 152). Where the braces cross, they are screwed together from beneath.

1 Position the first panel of one side wall on the decking (see left) and check that it is vertical. Drill pilot holes into the decking and joists below, and screw through the bottom batten with 4in x No.8 countersunk screws. Screw the other panel to the protruding battens.

2 Erect the first back panel, butting tightly up to the side wall, and screw the two together through the corner batten. Screw through the bottom batten into the decking and joists again, and fit the second panel. Repeat for the other two walls.

3 A view of the completed cross braces which are fixed in place with two 3in x No. 8 screws at each end. Where the braces intersect, they are joined with two 4in x No. 8 screws from the underside. This photo also shows the gable end and roof panels in position (see pages 151 and 152).

Fitting the gable ends

The gable ends are right-angled triangles and can be cut from one sheet of plywood. Draw a line across the centre of the sheet, to divide it into two squares, and draw one diagonal across each square. Cut out the four triangles with a jigsaw. Lay two of these triangles together to make up a gable end and cut a notch in the apex to take the 50 x 100 mm (2 x 4in) ridge board. Repeat for the other gable end.

We painted the gable ends with a drab grey opaque woodstain before cladding them with the hazel sticks when the stain had dried. These were fixed perpendicular to the bottom edge with panel pins. The simplest way to do this is to put on the hazel so it overhangs the plywood, and then to cut it off flush with a jigsaw. The hazel should be fairly dry, having been cut about six weeks previously, so that too much shrinkage does not occur.

Next fix the gable ends in position above the two side walls. In an ideal situation you can erect both gable ends and the ridge board, then fit the roof panels. Because of the position of our tree, we found it easier to erect only one half of the gable end adjacent to the tree, then fit the other half when one side of the roof had been boarded. This also had the advantage of giving the structure more rigidity. The side with no external decking next to it was awkward, and so we used a scaffold tower and tackled it with four people.

Position the gable end panels on top of the side wall and check that they are vertical with a spirit level, then fix them by screwing through the overlapping batten attached to the side panel, using 1½in x No. 8 screws at about 300mm (12in) centres. As they are not secure, fixed in this way, temporarily prop them with battens nailed to one of the cross braces. Join the two half gable end panels together with a vertical batten overlapping the joint. To provide fixings for the roof panels, screw two battens to the inside of each gable end panel, flush with the top edges.

1 After notching the apex of the gable end panels to take the ridge beam and coating them with woodstain, clad the panels with hazel coppice. Overlap the sticks at both edges and pin them in place using one to three 25-38mm (1-1½in) panel pins per stick, depending on length and thickness.

2 As you progress, trim off the overlapping ends flush with the edges of the triangle using a jigsaw, to allow the sticks to lie close to each other. Press down on the hazel as you do so.

3 The ridge board is connected to the gable end panels by two roof truss clips, nailed 18mm (¾in) in from each end. Position the gable end panel on top of the side wall, fit the notch in the panel round the ridge board, and screw the clip to the plywood with ½in screws.

4 Fix the gable end panel in position by screwing through the top wall batten, and join the two half panels together through the overlapping vertical batten. However carefully you plan, the unforeseen can always happen: the irregularly shaped cutout was necessary to avoid removing a large bough from the tree, but was made waterproof by the later addition of roofing felt.

Boarding the roof

The roof is boarded with plywood. Each side measures 1825 x 2440mm (72 x 96in) and is made up of one whole sheet and one cut sheet, fixed together with a batten. Screw the 2390mm (94in) connecting batten to one long side of the whole sheet of plywood, 25mm (1in) in from each end, with half its width protruding. To prevent the panel from sliding down during fixing – and to help position it – we fixed two temporary triangular blocks of wood, 40mm (1½in) in from each end and 113mm (4½in) up from the bottom edge, to act as stops against the top of the wall.

We attached a rope around the plywood sheet, and four people lifted it into position by going up the ladder and through the gap between the cross braces.

The two part sheets of plywood, which meet at the ridge, are 605 x 2440mm (24 x 96in). To make a neat join at the ridge, you can set the saw to cut at 45 degrees to the surface and then turn one sheet over so that the cut edges meet. Screw each sheet to the connecting batten, the fixing battens on the gable ends and the ridge board.

1 Position the lower roof panel square to the gable ends and overhanging the wall by 100mm (4in). Screw through the panel into battens fixed flush with the edges of the gable end panel at each end, and into horizontal battens fixed along the top of the wall and butting up to the roof panel. The upper roof panel is joined to the lower one by a batten running along the length, and is additionally screwed to the ridge board.

2 The roof is supported by a crown post, which fits between the lower cross brace and the ridge board, and two struts which run from each side of the crown post to the connecting battens joining the upper and lower roof panels. Cut the ends of the struts to the angle of the roof at the top and to meet the edge of the crown post at the bottom, and screw the supports in position.

Thatching the roof

To make the roof waterproof, we covered the plywood panels with roofing felt fixed with felt nails at about 300mm (12in) centres along the edges. One width of felt was taken along the bottom of the roof, flush with the bottom edge and overlapping the gable ends by 75mm (3in). Another width overlapped the first one by 75mm (3in) and was taken 100mm (4in) over the ridge. The same was repeated for the other side of the roof.

Two barge boards on each gable end secure the overlapping felt and form a finishing edge for the thatch. They are cut at an angle of 45 degrees where they meet in the centre. The lower ends of the barge boards project 50mm (2in) beyond the roof panels, and the top edges are proud of the felt by the same amount. We fixed each board with ten 75mm (3in) annular ringshank nails. When you fit the boards is not critical, providing they are in place when the thatch reaches them.

We put on the willow 'thatch' working from a ladder resting flat on the roof (and so at 45 degrees to the ground). To secure the bundles of willow, hammer in three rows of 20mm (¾in) galvanized staples: 250mm (10in) from the top and bottom edge of the roof; and midway between them. Space the staples at 50mm (2in) centres.

The thatching is a job for two people: one making up bundles of six willow lengths with the thin end uppermost, and passing them up to the thatcher who wires them to the staples. Lay the willow with the thin ends oversailing the ridge of the roof by 400mm (16in). The bottom ends also oversail but by random amounts. Starting at the top, tie the bundle to a staple in each row using green plastic-covered wire. Take the wire over and round the bundle and tie it in. Position another bundle beside it and tie it to the previous bundle and to the next staple, and so on across the roof. When several have been tied in, cut the bottom end of the bundles with secateurs to leave a small but consistent overhang of about 50mm (2in). The idea of the willow is to hide the felt, using as small an amount of willow as necessary. The top will be more gappy than the bottom as the stems are thinner here but, because the tops will be bent over to the other side, do not be concerned if a fair bit of felt shows through in the ridge area.

It is best to progress with the thatch on both sides of the roof together. Every few bundles, bend over the tops and wire them in to the corresponding staple on the opposite side of the roof. Trim off the ends 50mm (2in) below the wires.

Finally, cut six 7.5m (25ft) lengths of the rope (three times the length of the roof) and lay them treble over each line of wire and staples to hide them. Fix the rope in place with loops of wire attached to galvanized nails. You could cover the centre join between the bargeboards by nailing two diamond-shaped pieces from the same timber over them.

Finishing the platform

We cut balustrade spindles from 950mm (38in) long planks. The wavy edges were drawn freehand, the outside waves just touching the edges of the plank and the other lines parallel to them about 38mm (1½in) away.

1 Thatch the roof with bundles of six lengths of willow, with the thinner end uppermost. Starting at the top, tie the bundles to a staple in each row with plastic-coated garden wire. The bundle should project above the ridge by 400mm (16in) and at the bottom by about 75mm (3in) – to be trimmed later.

2 Trim the bottom end of the willow with secateurs to give a vertical 'edge', overhanging the eaves by about 50mm (2in). Leave the willow projecting above the ridge.

3 Before laying the last few bundles, nail the second pair of barge boards in position, projecting above the roof by 50mm (2in). Fix each board with ten 75mm (3in) annular ringshank nails; these have serrated shanks and grip very firmly, preventing the barge boards from pulling away.

1 Fix the spindles to the balustrade rails with two 3in screws per rail, so that the bottom ends of the spindles are 20mm (¾in) above the decking. The maximum gap between the spindles should not exceed 100mm (4in). Screw an additional spindle to each balustrade post (two to each corner post).

4 Bend the projecting ends of each bundle over the ridge and wire it into the top row of staples on the other side. Trim off the ends 50mm (2in) below the wire.

5 A view of the ridge thatch, showing the willow on the near side of the roof bent over and tied down on the far side, and the willow from the far side (partly completed) tied in to the top row of staples.

6 Cover the wires with manilla rope, secured every 300mm (12in). Attach one end of a 150mm (6in) length of galvanized wire to a 50mm (2in) galvanized nail and hammer it into the roof board on one side of the ropes. Attach a small loop of wire to a second nail and hammer this in on the other side of the ropes. Pass the free end of wire over the ropes, thread it through the loop and twist to secure it.

2 Cut the fascia boards from bark-edged spruce and nail them to the platform using 75mm (3in) annular ringshank nails, with the top edge flush with the surface of the decking. The front and back fascia boards overlap the ends of the side fascia boards.

Doors and windows

Returning to the doors that you cut out of the front wall panels, first cut 10mm (⅜in) off the bottom edge of each to give clearance above the decking. Cut out the windows with a jigsaw, leaving a 100mm (4in) wide band around the edge.

We clad the doors with wavy softwood planks; this would also be a suitable way to clad the sides of the house, if preferred. Pin the planks 3mm (⅛in) apart to the outer face of the door with 25mm (1in) panel pins. Overlap the window opening by about 10mm (⅜in), leaving the planks wavy, to form a rebate for the glazing. Trim the cladding to the contours of the door.

Make the trellis for the windows from prepared-all-round (PAR) batten. On a piece of scrap plywood, trace the outline of one of the windows in the doors. Draw lines on it at 100mm (4in) centres, at 45 degrees to the bottom line, projecting beyond the window outline. Cut lengths of batten to fit centrally on these lines and mark their ends to the angle of the window outline where they cross it. Label each batten and its corresponding line on the board with a letter of the alphabet, so that they can be repositioned in the same order, then draw a random, wavy, pencil line on each edge of the battens before cutting them out with a jigsaw. Replace the battens in the correct position on the board and fix them together with a panel pin at each junction. Before fixing them in the windows, paint them with two coats of Oxan woodstain.

Before hanging the doors, strengthen the plywood around the entrance by fixing a stiffener flush with each edge of the opening and a horizontal one above the apex. Notch the side ones to fit over the bottom wall batten and butt them up to the top wall batten. Fix each stiffener with four 2in screws, screwing through the wall plywood into the timber. The side stiffeners also provide a mounting for the door hinges; when the doors are hung, the surface of the door cladding should be flush with the outer surface of the front wall panels. To enable the doors to swing freely, chisel out a 2mm (⁵⁄₆₄in) deep recess in the doors and stiffeners around the hinge knuckles.

Decide which door will be the first to open and fit a gate latch to it. Fit a bolt to the inside of the other door, shooting downwards into a blind hole drilled in the decking. Glaze the windows with clear acrylic sheet, fixed in position with silicone mastic. Use the same procedure for the Gothic window in the side wall.

1 Mark out the windows in the door panels, and check that the labelling relating them to the wall panels will still be in place when the window is cut out. Drill a starting hole for the jigsaw blade within the marked lines and cut out the window openings. Work into the corners from both angles to remove the waste.

2 The doors were clad with sawn planks of softwood about 850mm (34in) long, working from left to right across the door. Draw a freehand wavy line as close as possible to the right-hand edge of the first length. Cut this out with a jigsaw and use it as a template for the left-hand edge of the next plank. Continue in this way across the door.

3 Mark the hinge positions on the inner face of the door, 230mm (9in) below the base of the arch and the same distance up from the bottom edge. The hinge knuckle should align with the edge of the door. Drill pilot holes and screw the hinges in place.

4 Before hanging the doors, make the trellis for the windows. Set out the battens on a marked-out baseboard. Mark and cut the ends to shape and label each piece. Then cut the wavy edges with a jigsaw.

5 Join the trellis pieces with 20mm (¾in) panel pins where they overlap. Pin the completed trellis into the edge of the rebate formed by the overlapping door cladding.

6 Using a handyman's knife, score the clear acrylic sheeting for the windows, making sure it is fractionally smaller than the opening. Cut along the scored lines with a jigsaw. Ensure that the sheet is well supported close to the cutting position, otherwise it is likely to crack.

7 Squeeze a bead of clear multi-purpose silicone sealant along each of the inner layer of battens.

8 Press the acrylic sheet on to the battens, and apply a continuous bead of the silicone round the edges of the pane.

9 Fit the latch keeper to the door with the bolt, and the latch itself to the inside of the other door. Drill a hole for the latch spindle, pass the spindle through the door, and screw the ring handle over it on the outside.

Cladding

We used two different types of cladding for the walls, and the wavy cladding used on the doors is a further option. Before applying the cladding, we painted the walls in the same opaque drab grey woodstain.

The front wall was clad with beech log discs of 50 to 150mm (2 to 6in) diameter, cut with a chainsaw to about 20mm (¾in) thick. (See page 118 for chainsaw safety.) Pin the discs to the wall (working from one side to the other) so that each disc butts up to its neighbours. Allow the discs

to overhang the doorway slightly to soften the shape and to provide a doorstop for the doors, which open inwards.

The back and side walls of the house were clad with barked strips about 2m (6ft 6in) long. Working from the bottom upwards, nail them to the ply with about eight oval nails per length. Fix two whole lengths at one side of the wall then cut lengths to fill the remaining space. Start the next two rows with the whole lengths at the other side of the wall so that the joints between lengths are staggered.

Another cladding option is moulded log rounds. The plain white, moulded sheet has the surface texture of logs of wood, complete with bark and knots. It could be mounted horizontally, vertically or at an angle. The sheet was first sprayed matt black, using cellulose car-body paint. When this had dried, we sprayed it randomly with grey and yellow cellulose paint to leave a patchy colouration. Other colours of acrylic paint were then applied by brush to give the appearance of tree bark, lichens and algae. Secure the panels with beads of gap-filling adhesive.

BEFORE   **AFTER**

key to suppliers

Note: Many items are available ready-made from www.bunnyguinness.com

Awning
- Pine poles from R.L. Trim
- Finials from Thornwood Designs
- Mast bands from Timber Intent
- Wooden tension adjusters from R.L. Trim
- Tent pegs from R.L. Trim
- Cotton rope from Footrope Knots
- Gold paint, Judson's, from Crosbie Coatings Ltd

Chequerboard paving
- Indian stone slabs from Stone Age International

Compost bins
- Railway sleepers, imported hardwood, from Atlantic
- Woodstain, Jotun's Demidekk, for softwood board option only

False stone window
- Vacuum-formed Gothic window from Peter Evans Studios
- Woodstain, Jotun's Demidekk
- Timber from Atlantic

Finials
- Artichoke: pvc mould from Peter Evans Studio
- Pine cone: terracotta finial from Deroma UK Ltd
- Metal 'spade': metal 'spade' finial from Artistic Ironwork Supplies Ltd, and aluminium leaf from C. Cornelissen and Sons Ltd
- Wooden finial: hardwood finial from Paul Procter, of Thornwood Designs; blue opaque woodstain (3121-R99B), Jotun's Demidekk; metallic paints from Polyvine
- Fleur-de-lis: pvc mould from Peter Evans Studio

Galvanized steel planter
- Galvanized steel sheet (ideally from offcuts) from blacksmith, see local telephone directory
- Mild steel edging section from FH Brundle Expanding Metals

Grass steps
- Paving slabs from Stone Age International

Herb cloche
- Timber from Atlantic

Mosaic paving
- Indian stone paving setts, from Stone Age International
- Mixed colour pebbles from CED
- Snowdonia tumbled pebbles, from Pinks Hill Nursery

Oak table and benches
- Green oak from Harry Adcock Ltd
- Stainless steel fixings, from boat chandlers, see local telephone directory

Plant labels
- Slate label: slate labels from John Finnemore and Sons
- Plastic label: soft green plastic label from Wells and Winter, Kent
- Aluminium label with stamped letters: letter stamps from Smith Francis Tools Ltd
- Aluminium label with self-adhesive letters: lettering machines from The Touch Labelling Company

Rustic cupboard
- Cedar from C.N. Spencer Ltd
- Other timber from Atlantic

Sculpture in a hedge
- Moulded plastic portrait head available from Peter Evans Studio
- Verdigris paints available from Polyvine

Serpentine mowing margin
- Indian stone slabs from Stone Age International

Shell wall fountain
- Large codestone ammonite (mentioned in the introduction on page 58) from Thomason Cudworth
- Shells from Marine Arts
- Pebbles from CED
- Pump from Hozelock
- Timber from Atlantic

Sundial
- The British Sundial Society
- Sun face in ABS from Peter Evans Studios
- Gold leaf and size from C. Cornelissen and Sons Ltd
- Timber from Atlantic

Teenagers' treehouse
- Rustic softwood planks with bark edging from Lincolnshire Woodcraft Supplies
- Gable ends: coppiced hazel twigs, from J.R. Harnan
- Thatch: willow cuttings (Salix viminalis or similar), from Nene Park Trust
- Manilla rope from Footrope Knots
- Woodstain, Jotun's Oxan colour Antikk (for 'ageing' wood)
- Timber from Atlantic

Timber and steel planter
- Galvanized steel sheet from blacksmith, see local telephone directory
- Timber ball finials from Thornwood Designs
- Timber from Atlantic

Timber balustrade
- Oval finials with plinth from Thornwood Designs
- Woodstain, Jotun's Demidekk, or similar
- Timber from Atlantic

Trampoline
- Trampoline from Supertramp

Tree seat
- Woodstain, opaque dark green (BS 12B25), Jotun's Demidekk
- Timber from Atlantic

Trellis hedge house
- Finials, 65mm timber balls with dowels, from Thornwood Designs
- Jotun's Demidekk opaque woodstain or similar
- Timber from Atlantic

Trompe l'oeil arbour
- Reconstituted stone seat from www.bunnyguinness.com
- Opaque woodstain, Jotun's Demidekk
- Timber from Atlantic

Trompe l'oeil doors
- Opaque woodstain, Jotun's Demidekk
- Timber from Atlantic

Woven archway
- Metal archway, made up by a blacksmith, see local telephone directory
- Willow wands, Salix vitellina, from Nene Park Trust

Woven oak strip fencing
- Oak strips, from Lincolnshire Woodcraft Supplies
- Willow wands, Salix vitellina, from Nene Park Trust

Woven tree seat
- Water-permeable membrane, Mypex, from garden centres
- Hazel poles from J.R. Harnan
- Willow wands, Salix vitellina, from Nene Park Trust

suppliers

Harry Adcock Ltd., The Saw Mill, Old Station Yard, Corby Glen, Grantham, Lincs NG33 4LB Tel 01476 550231
Plant labels: oak labels; Oak table and benches: timber

Artistic Ironwork Supplies
Edwin Avenue, Hoo Farm Industrial Estate, Worcester Road, Kidderminster, Worcestershire DY11 7RA Tel 01562 825252 Fax 01562 820380
Finials: metal 'spade' finial

Atlantic – The Country Superstore, The Old Mill, Earsham, Bungay, Suffolk NR35 2QT Tel 01986 894745 Fax 01986 892496
Mail order service; supplies a wide range of timber, plywoods, sleepers, telegraph poles, ironmongery, fencing etc. Supplied general timber for most projects, see opposite for details

British Sundial Society, Mr D A Bateman, 4 New Wokingham Road, Crowthorne, Berkshire RG45 7NR Tel 01344 772303; website www.sundials.co.uk/bsshome.htm

FH Brundle Expanding Metals, Unit 3, Eldon Road Industrial Estate, Attenborough, Nottingham, NG9 6RB Tel 0115 9430505 Fax 0115 9430831
Galvanized steel planter: Mild steel edging section

C. Cornelissen & Sons Ltd, 105 Great Russell Street, London WC1B 3RY. Tel 020 76361045
Mail order. Sundial: gold leaf and size; Metal 'spade' finial: aluminium leaf

CED, 728 London Road, West Thurrock, Grays, Essex RM20 3LU Tel 01708 867237 Fax 01708 867230
Mosaic paving: mixed colour pebbles; Wall fountain: pebbles

Crosbie Coatings Ltd., Walsall Street, Wolverhampton WV1 3LP Tel 01902 352020 Fax 01902 456392
Awning: Judson's gold paint

Deroma UK Ltd, Unit 14 Quedgeley Trading Estate East, Haresfield, Stonehouse, Gloucestershire GL10 3EX Tel 01452 725520 Fax 01452 725521
Pinecone finial: terracotta finial

Peter Evans Studios Ltd, 1 Frederick Street, Luton, Beds LU2 7QW. Tel 01582 725730 Fax 01582 481329
False stone window: ABS vacuum-formed window

moulding (PE553 1.2ABS), also architectural features; Sculpture in a hedge: Angelo, TSI; Finials: artichoke and fleur de lis; Sundial: sun face

John Finnemore and Sons, The White House, Glaston Road, Uppingham, Oakham Rutland LE15 9EU.
Tree seat: reconstituted stone balls

Footrope Knots, 501 Wherstead Road, Ipswich, Suffolk IP2 8LL. Tel 01473 690090
Awning: cotton rope; Teenager's treehouse: manilla rope

J.R. Harnan, 3 Reedings Close, Barrowby, Nr. Grantham, Lincs NG32 1AX Tel 01476 574531
Woven tree seat and Woven archway: hazel; Teenager's treehouse: coppiced hazel twigs

Hozelock Ltd, Haddenham, Aylesbury, Buckinghamshire HP17 8JD Tel 01844 292002
Shell wall fountain: water pump

Jotun-Henry Clark Ltd, Stather Road, Flixborough, Scunthorpe, North Lincolnshire DN15 8RR Tel 01724 400123 Fax 01724 400130
Various projects: woodstains, an extremely wide colour range of translucent and opaque stains

Lincolnshire Woodcraft Supplies, The Old Sawmills, Burghley Park, London Road, Stamford PE9 3JX Tel 01780 757825
Woven oak strip fencing: oak strips; Compost bins: rustic poles; Teenagers' treehouse: rustic poles and log rounds

Marine Arts Ltd., The Shell Factory, Long Rock, Penzance, Cornwall, TR20 8HX Tel 01736 365169 Fax 01736 368545
Shell wall fountain: shells

Nene Park Trust, Ham Farm House, Ham Lane, Peterborough PE2 5UU Tel 01733 234193 Fax 01733 361342
Woven archway, Woven tree seat and Woven oak strip fencing: willow wands; Teenagers' treehouse: willow for roof

Pinks Hill Nursery (Landscape Merchants), Wood Street Village, Guildford, Surrey, GU3 3BP Tel 01483 571620 Fax 01483 536816
Mosaic paving: Snowdonia tumbled pebbles

Polyvine Ltd., Vine House, Rockhampton, Berkeley, Glos GL13 9DT Tel 01454 261276 Fax 01454 261286
Sculpture in a hedge: verdigris paints

Smith Francis Tools Ltd, Priory Works, 66 Moseley Street, Birmingham B12 0RT Tel 0121 6223311 Fax 0121 6667201
Aluminium plant label: letter punches

C.N. Spencer Ltd
Sudborough Road, Brigstock, Kettering NN14 3HP
Rustic cupboard: cedar timber

Stone Age International, 1 Rycroft Avenue, Deeping St. James, Peterborough, PE6 8NT Tel 01778 342567 Fax 01778 422933
Chequerboard paving, Grass steps and Serpentine mowing margin: Indian stone slabs; mosaic paving: Indian stone setts

Supertramp, Langlands Business Park, Uffculme, Cullompton, Devon, EX15 3DA Tel 01884 841305
Trampoline. Will also supply muted green edge for trampoline

Thomason Cudworth, The Old Vicarage, Cudworth, Ilminster, Somerset TA9 0PR Tel 01460 57322
Ammonites

Thornwood Designs, Paul Procter, Unit 6, Top factory, Cringle Lane, Stoke Rochford, Grantham NG33 5EF Tel 01476 530600
Will make any shape or size of finial to order. Awning: onion-shaped finials; Timber balustrade: oval finials with plinth; Timber and steel planter: timber ball finials

Timber Intent Ltd, 32 Belton Road, Bristol BS5 0J6 Tel 0117 939 6948
Awning: mast bands (gunmetal and aluminium)

The Touch Labelling Co, Unit 10, Buntsford Hill Business Park, Buntsford Park Road, Bromsgrove B60 3DX Tel 01527 574910 Fax 01527 575037
Plant labels: machine is P Touch 8000. The labels are self laminating and UV stable. More affordable versions of the label printing machine are available for the amateur garden.

R. L. Trim, Acreman Street, Cerne Abbas, Dorchester, Dorset, DT2 7LD Tel 01300 341209 Fax 01300 341 815
Tent manufacturer. Awning: poles, pegs and tension adjusters or wood slips

Wells & Winter, Mereworth, Maidstone, Kent ME18 5NB Tel 01622 813627
Plant labels: soft green plastic label

index

acknowledgements

I would like to express my sincere thanks to the people who have assisted me in the production of this book. In particular I would like to thank the following: John Courton, David Harrison and Martin Rodgers for their help in building the numerous projects and for their advice, ideas and views on many details; and Mike Trier, the technical editor, who managed to keep us all on the straight and narrow but still remained fun to work with. Special thanks are due to Colin Leftley, the photographer, who somehow managed to work through long days with freezing fingers during the winter months and yet produced great pictures. He showed quite an aptitude for DIY at critical junctures!

I would also like to thank Bet Ayer, the art director for her creativity, and Anna Mumford, the editor, for pulling the whole book together.

Finally I would like to thank my husband and children who put up with months of hammering, banging and drilling while their home and garden were turned into a workshop.